Tarot by Design
WORKBOOK

color and learn your way into the cards

Diana Heyne

WEISER BOOKS

This edition first published in 2017 by Weiser Books, an imprint of
Red Wheel/Weiser, LLC

With offices at:
65 Parker Street, Suite 7
Newburyport, MA 01950
www.redwheelweiser.com

ISBN: 978-1-57863-607-5

Cover design by Jim Warner

Printed in the United States of America
M&G

10 9 8 7 6 5 4 3 2 1

DEDICATED WITH LOVE AND RESPECT
TO ALL THE MAGICAL WOMEN
IN MY FAMILY TREE

INTRODUCTION

have long felt that many people hesitate to set foot on the path of Tarot because even the initial steps can appear somewhat daunting. Familiarizing oneself with the images and numbers for seventy-eight cards and getting a grasp of both their upright and reversed meanings can seem difficult or bring back unpleasant memories of having to learn by rote long lists of facts and dates for school. No matter how alluring or beneficial learning the Tarot might seem to us, there is always this hurdle to be gotten over before one even begins the task of making sense of the cards' interactions within a reading.

I believe there is a better and more enjoyable way to learn the basics of the Tarot cards. When we engage our visual and kinesthetic senses through the movement of applying color to these images, learning, informed by intuition, takes on a friendlier face. This book offers coloring-ready versions of the cards, each accompanied by a learning page. The very best way to familiarize yourself with the symbolic and visual language of the cards is to enter into them through the process of applying color (and a pattern if you like) to each.

To begin, spend a moment really looking at and noticing the details and emotional tone of each image. Who are the characters in the image? What seems to be happening? How does it make you feel? What objects or props are depicted? What is the setting or environment? What stories can you imagine involving these characters and places?

Adding color provides a way to enhance and underscore the meaning of the cards and in the process, allows us to pass into a calmer, more contemplative state of mind where the voice of our intuition can be heard more clearly. Don't feel bound by any set of rules for making your color choices. We all have a personal color palette of likes and dislikes, color associations and connotations that can make one color appealing while another is emotionally troubling. Whole books and websites have been devoted to the esoteric and symbolic significance of color but, in successfully dealing with the Tarot, your personal understanding of color will provide the most resonance with the cards and thus, create more effective learning.

Accompanying each card is a learning page with several short written meanings for that card in upright and reversed positions. (And yes, you have to physically reverse the page to easily read the reversed meanings!) These brief notes are designed so that they can be colored in a way to impress the written information into memory by highlighting individual words or phrases with different colors and perhaps, adding a pattern around each. There is also room to record your own impressions and ideas or to make small thumbnail sketches if you like or even to create a collage of images or printed words.

For all twenty-two of the major arcana cards, the learning page also contains a short rhyme or phrase that briefly encompasses the most important aspects of each image and may provide another route to recalling what the cards signify, in much the same way that song lyrics or commercial jingles can easily be absorbed and remain clearly lodged in our memories.

A vast array of books and websites are available to offer guidance in using the Tarot for readings and in deepening your understanding through related studies such as numerology, Kabbalah, or even Jungian psychology, to name but a few. But don't let the amount of information discourage you. You have in your hands the first steps needed to systematically and successfully embark upon an enjoyable journey down the royal road of Tarot. What you learn here will provide a foundation that can be built upon to deepen and expand your knowledge and reach whatever level you choose. It can be a most rewarding and enjoyable process, starting now.

Diana

Tarot by Design
WORKBOOK

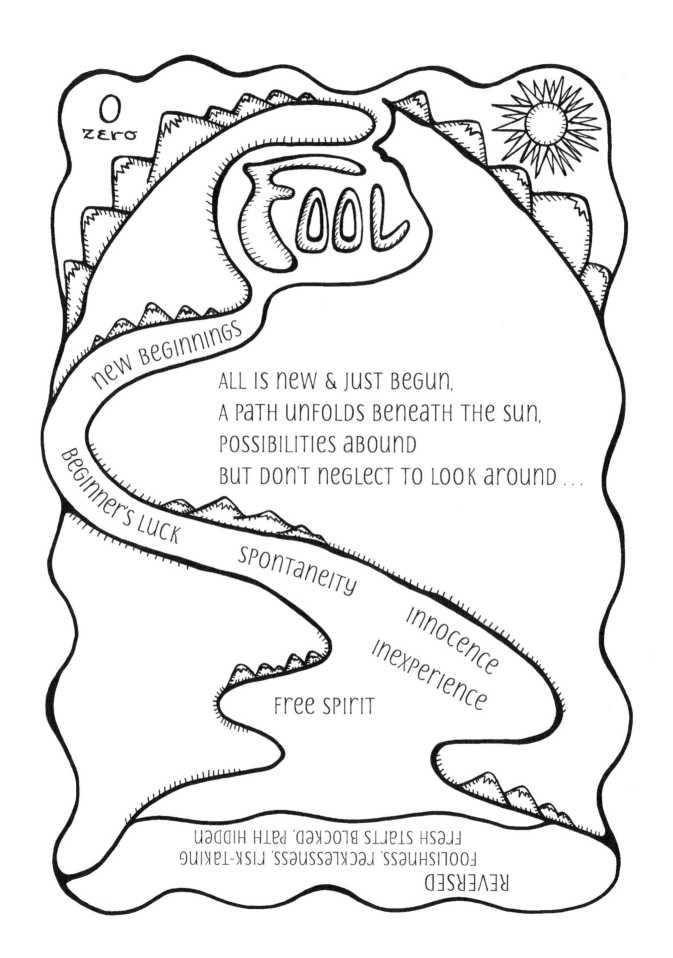

O zero

FOOL

new beginnings

ALL IS NEW & JUST BEGUN,
A PATH UNFOLDS BENEATH THE SUN,
POSSIBILITIES ABOUND
BUT DON'T NEGLECT TO LOOK AROUND . . .

BEGINNER'S LUCK

SPONTANEITY

INNOCENCE

INEXPERIENCE

FREE SPIRIT

REVERSED
FOOLISHNESS, RECKLESSNESS, RISK-TAKING
FRESH STARTS BLOCKED, PATH HIDDEN

MAGICIAN

BALANCE CONFIDENCE POWER SKILL

THE TOOLS TO CREATE

UNION BETWEEN HEAVEN & EARTH

ACTION MAGIC

The Balance Between earth & Heaven,
Lies WITHIN MY GRASP,
I POSSESS THE TOOLS,
I HOLD THE SKILL,
THE MAGIC KEY I CLASP . . .

NOTES:

REVERSED
unused talents, poor planning,
disgrace, manipulation

card ~ I ~ one

HIGH PRIESTESS

MYSTERY SECRETS HIDDEN KNOWLEDGE INTUITION

SILENCE WISDOM IMAGINATION SUBCONSCIOUS

I CONTAIN THE REALM OF SECRETS
INTUITION IS MY DWELLING PLACE
HIDDEN HEARTS & HIDDEN MINDS
ARE OPEN TO MY GRACE...

NOTES

REVERSED
SUPERFICIAL
BLOCKED INTUITION
NEED TO LISTEN TO INNER VOICE
HIDDEN AGENDA

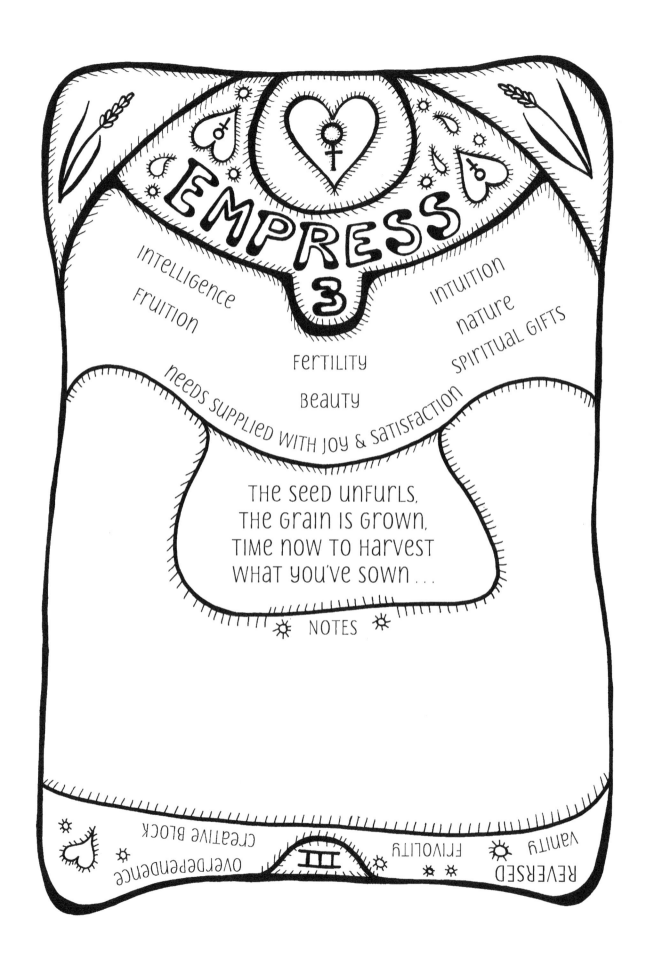

EMPRESS
3

INTELLIGENCE
FRUITION
INTUITION
nature
SPIRITUAL GIFTS
FERTILITY
BEAUTY
needs supplied with joy & satisfaction

THE SEED UNFURLS,
THE GRAIN IS GROWN,
TIME NOW TO HARVEST
WHAT YOU'VE SOWN...

NOTES

III

REVERSED
OVERDEPENDENCE   CREATIVE BLOCK   FRIVOLITY   vanity

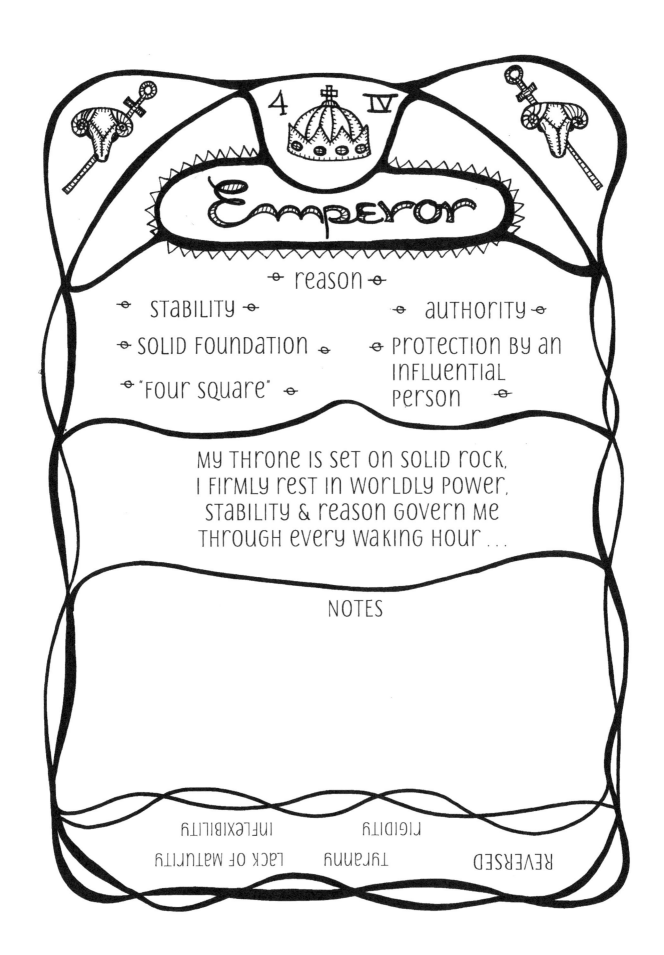

Emperor

4 IV

⊸ reason ⊶

⊸ STABILITY ⊶   ⊸ AUTHORITY ⊶

⊸ SOLID FOUNDATION ⊶   ⊸ PROTECTION BY AN INFLUENTIAL PERSON ⊶

⊸ "FOUR SQUARE" ⊶

MY THRONE IS SET ON SOLID ROCK,
I FIRMLY REST IN WORLDLY POWER,
STABILITY & REASON GOVERN ME
THROUGH EVERY WAKING HOUR . . .

NOTES

REVERSED   TYRANNY   RIGIDITY   LACK OF MATURITY   INFLEXIBILITY

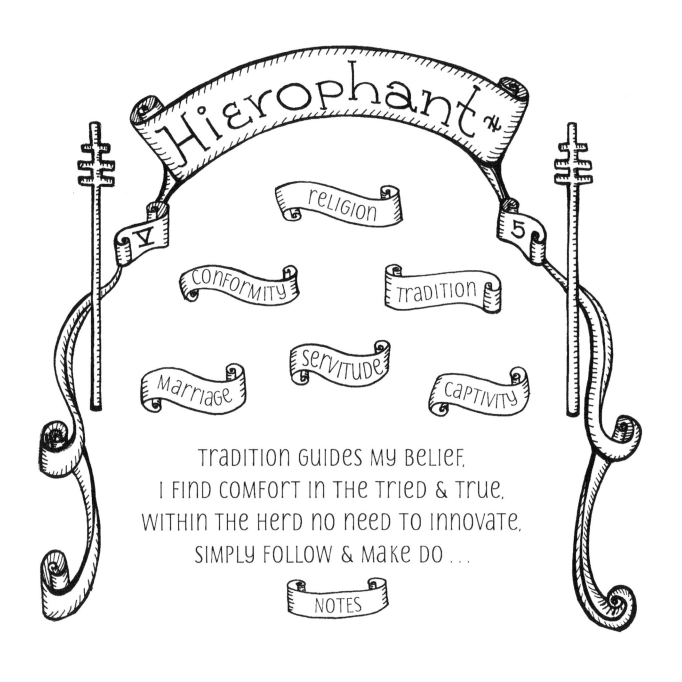

Hierophant

religion

conformity

tradition

servitude

marriage

captivity

Tradition guides my belief,
I find comfort in the tried & true,
Within the herd no need to innovate,
Simply follow & make do . . .

NOTES

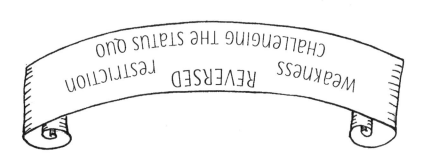

REVERSED
weakness
restriction
challenging the status quo

THE LOVERS

VI

~ BEAUTY ~

~ CHOICES ~

~ UNION ~

~ RELATIONSHIPS ~

LOVE'S SPELL IS SPUN,
A CHOICE IS MADE
TWO INTO ONE
THEIR UNION MAKE...

REVERSED
DISHARMONY, IMBALANCE

THE LOVERS
VI

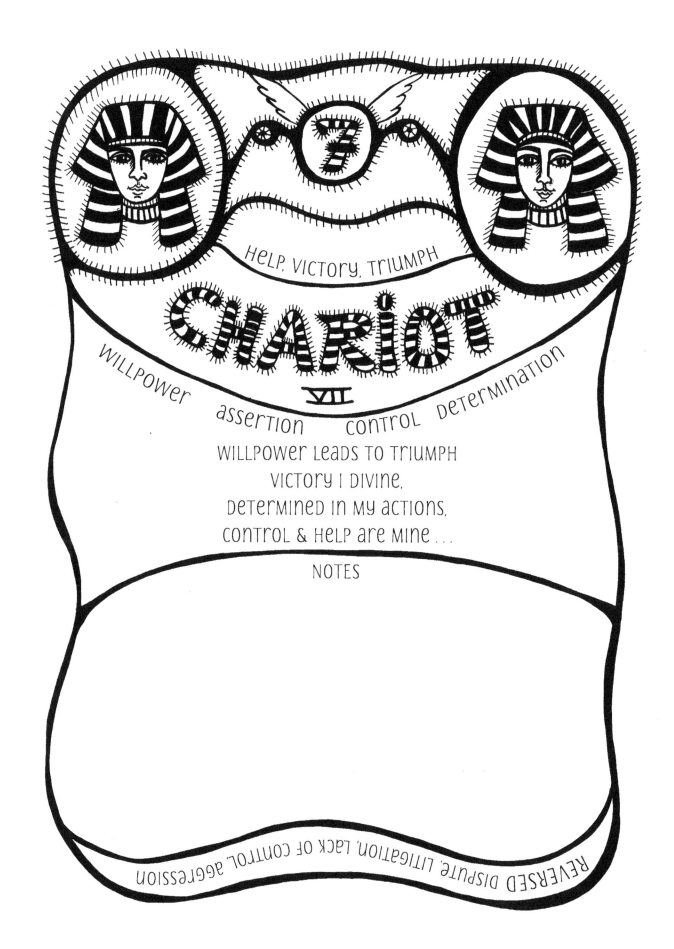

HELP, VICTORY, TRIUMPH

CHARIOT

VII

WILLPOWER   assertion   CONTROL   DETERMINATION

WILLPOWER LEADS TO TRIUMPH
VICTORY I DIVINE,
DETERMINED IN MY ACTIONS,
CONTROL & HELP ARE MINE...

NOTES

REVERSED DISPUTE, LITIGATION, LACK OF CONTROL, AGGRESSION

VIII

STRENGTH 8

POWER PATIENCE CONTROL
ENERGY COMPASSION ACTION
COURAGE

COURAGE AND COMPASSION
GUIDE THE ENERGY OF
ACTION...

NOTES

REVERSED

ABUSE OF POWER, FEEBLENESS, SELF-DOUBT,
WEAKNESS, LACK OF SELF-DISCIPLINE

THE HERMIT
IX

SOUL-SEARCHING

INTROSPECTION

SEEKING WISDOM

PRUDENCE

ALONE

I WALK A LONELY PATH,
ONLY MY LANTERN LIGHTS THE WAY.
I SEARCH FOR UNDERSTANDING,
I SEEK OUT WISDOM NIGHT & DAY.

NOTES:

FEAR

WITHDRAWAL

LONELINESS

ISOLATION

9

REVERSED

HERMIT IX

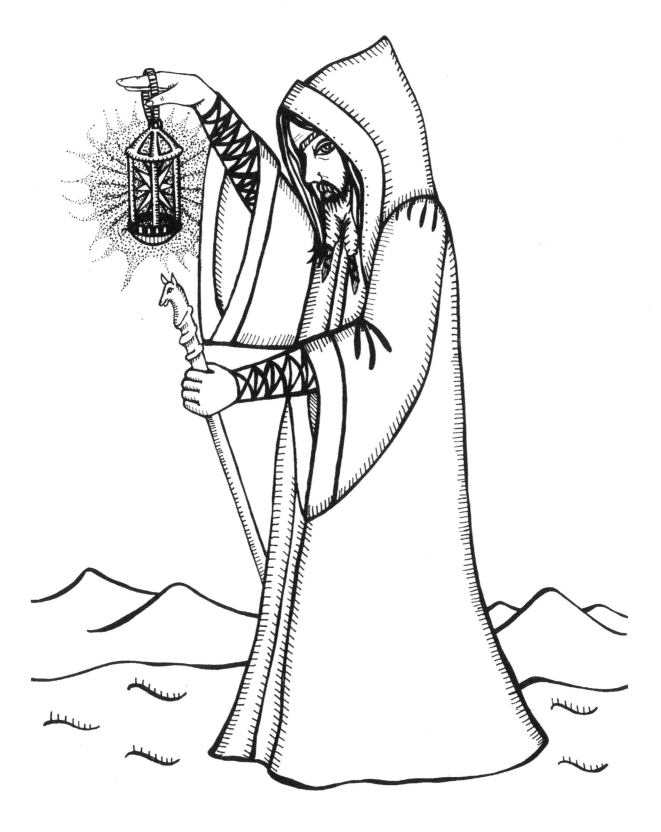

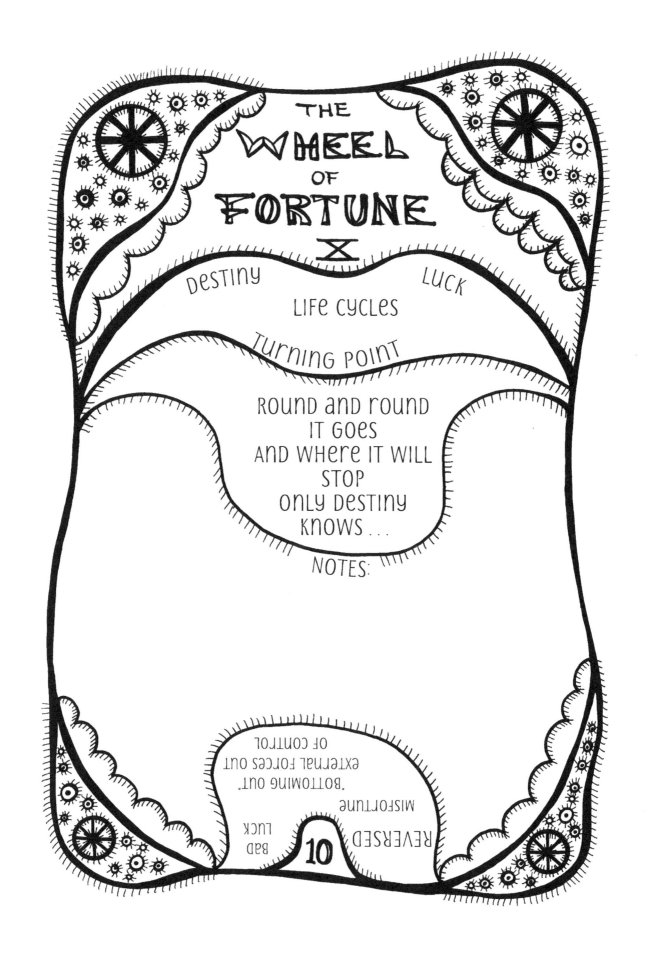

THE WHEEL OF FORTUNE
X

DESTINY   LUCK

LIFE CYCLES

TURNING POINT

ROUND AND ROUND
IT GOES
AND WHERE IT WILL
STOP
ONLY DESTINY
KNOWS . . .

NOTES:

REVERSED

BAD
LUCK

10

MISFORTUNE

"BOTTOMING OUT"

EXTERNAL FORCES OUT
OF CONTROL

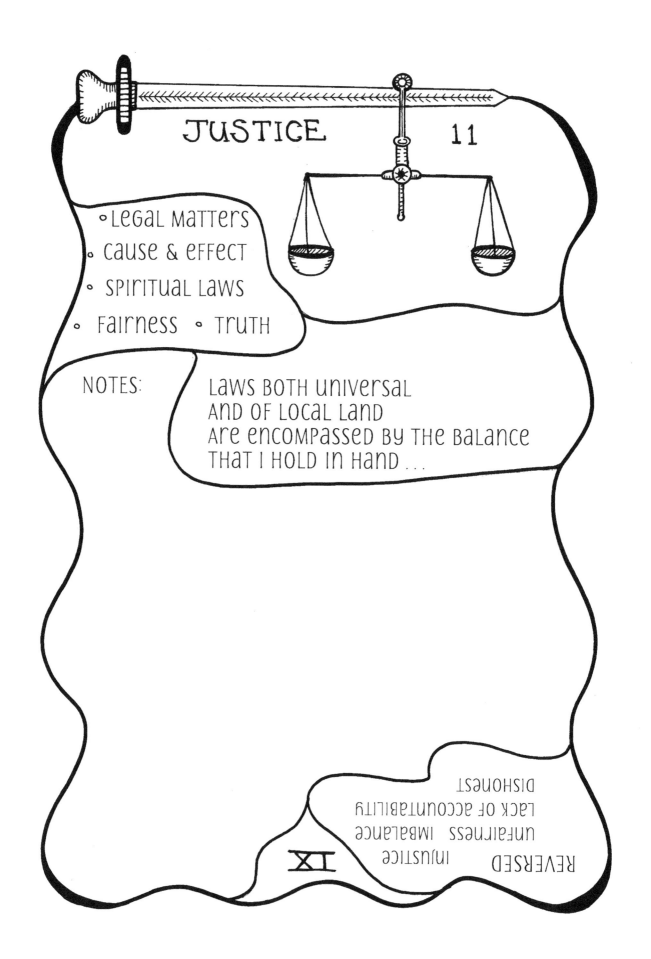

JUSTICE

11

- Legal Matters
- Cause & Effect
- Spiritual Laws
- Fairness • Truth

NOTES:

LAWS BOTH universal
AND OF LOCAL LAND
Are encompassed by the balance
THAT I HOLD IN HAND . . .

XI

REVERSED   injustice
unfairness   imbalance
Lack of accountability
dishonest

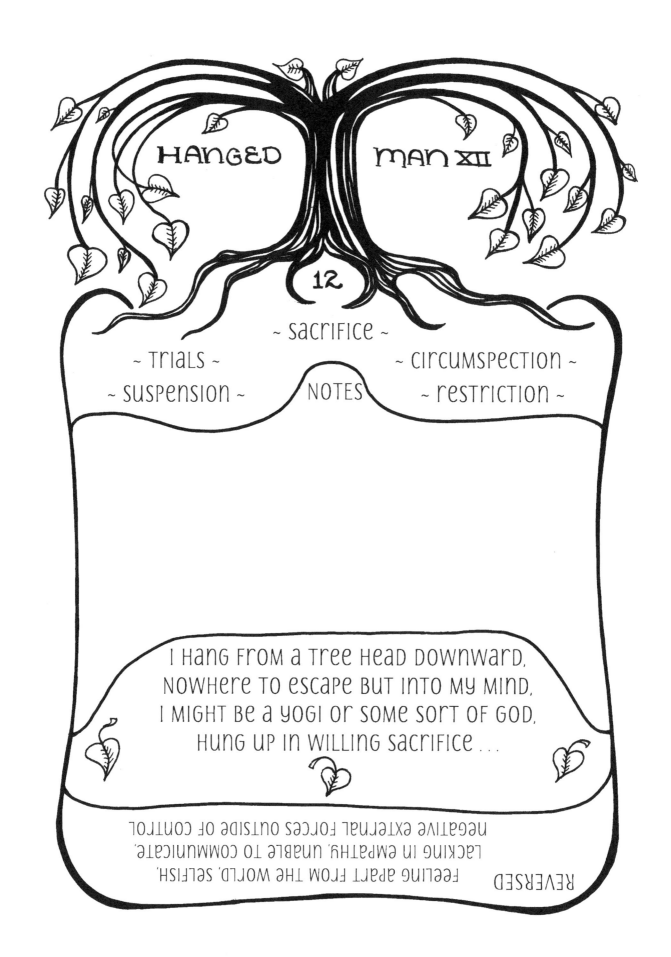

HANGED MAN XII

12

~ SACRIFICE ~

~ TRIALS ~   ~ CIRCUMSPECTION ~

~ SUSPENSION ~   NOTES   ~ RESTRICTION ~

I HANG FROM A TREE HEAD DOWNWARD,
NOWHERE TO ESCAPE BUT INTO MY MIND,
I MIGHT BE A YOGI OR SOME SORT OF GOD,
HUNG UP IN WILLING SACRIFICE . . .

REVERSED

FEELING APART FROM THE WORLD, SELFISH,
LACKING IN EMPATHY, UNABLE TO COMMUNICATE,
NEGATIVE EXTERNAL FORCES OUTSIDE OF CONTROL.

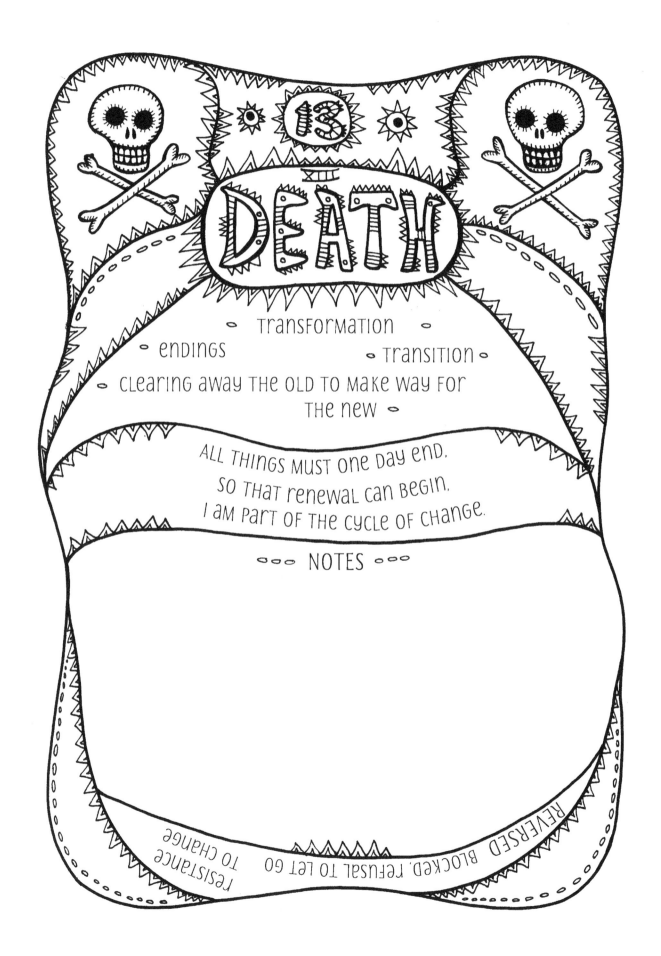

13

DEATH

- TRANSFORMATION
- ENDINGS
- TRANSITION
- CLEARING AWAY THE OLD TO MAKE WAY FOR THE NEW

ALL THINGS MUST ONE DAY END,
SO THAT RENEWAL CAN BEGIN.
I AM PART OF THE CYCLE OF CHANGE.

ooo NOTES ooo

REVERSED: BLOCKED, REFUSAL TO LET GO, RESISTANCE TO CHANGE

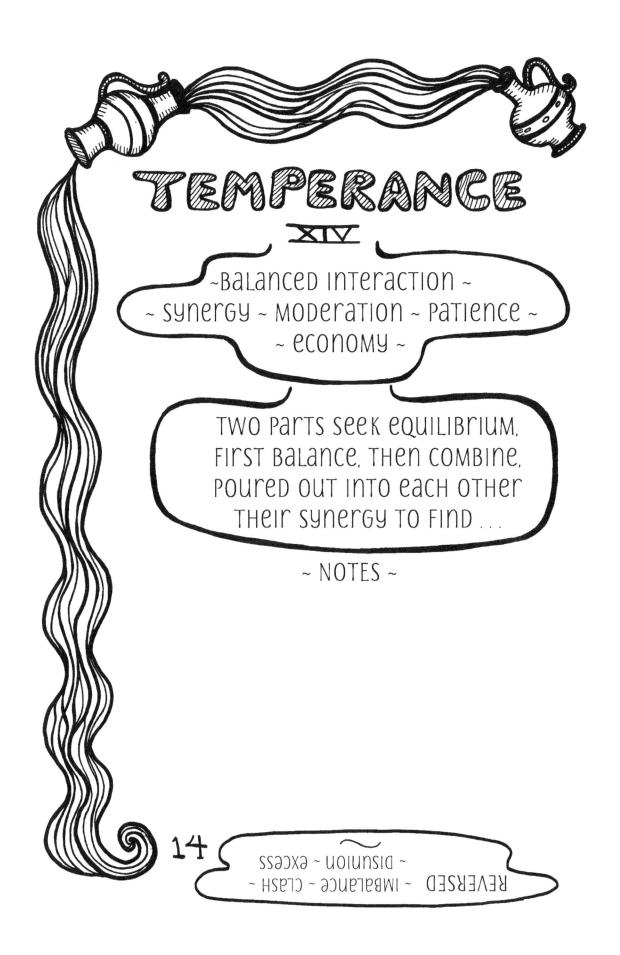

TEMPERANCE

XIV

~ BALANCED INTERACTION ~
~ SYNERGY ~ MODERATION ~ PATIENCE ~
~ ECONOMY ~

TWO PARTS SEEK EQUILIBRIUM,
FIRST BALANCE, THEN COMBINE,
POURED OUT INTO EACH OTHER
THEIR SYNERGY TO FIND . . .

~ NOTES ~

14

REVERSED ~ IMBALANCE ~ CLASH ~
~ DISUNION ~ EXCESS

XV

THE DEVIL

⭐ MATERIALISM
✴ BONDAGE
✴ ADDICTION

⭐ PRIMAL SOURCE OF DESIRES & EARTHLY NEEDS
✴ COMPULSIVE BEHAVIOR

I'LL LAUGH AT YOUR ADDICTIONS, ALL YOUR STRANGE, COMPELLING PREDILICTIONS, MY CHAINS YOU PUT ON WILLINGLY. I AM THE ROOT OF EARTHLY DESIRES— HOW TEDIOUS LIFE WITHOUT ME WOULD BE . . .

NOTES

REVERSED

LACK OF DESIRES OR DRIVE, TEMPTATION RESISTED, RESTRICTIVE MORALS, POWER RECLAIMED

15

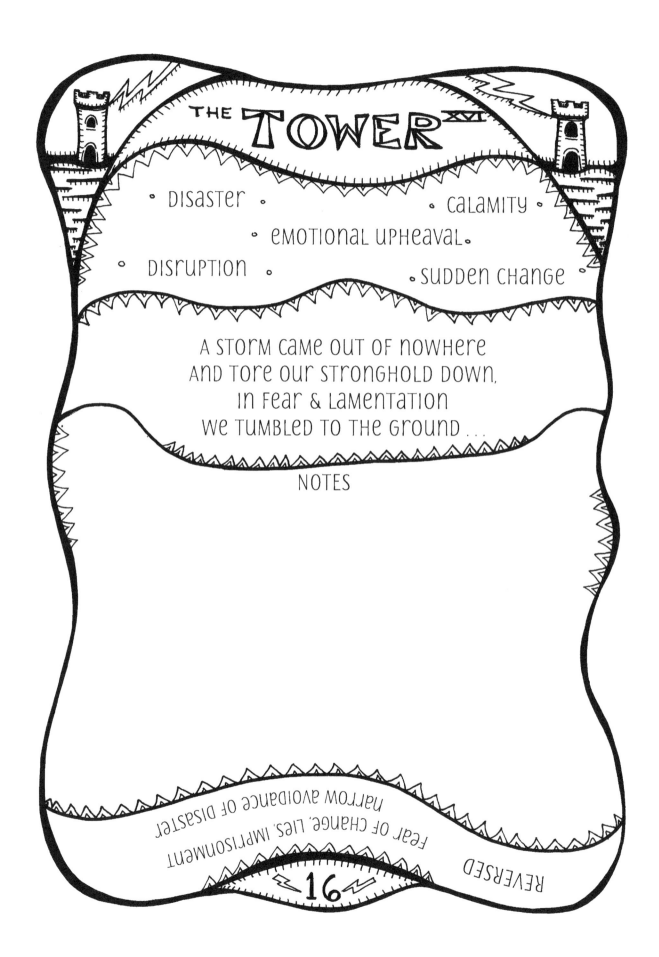

THE **TOWER** XVI

- DISASTER
- CALAMITY
- EMOTIONAL UPHEAVAL
- DISRUPTION
- SUDDEN CHANGE

A STORM CAME OUT OF NOWHERE
AND TORE OUR STRONGHOLD DOWN,
IN FEAR & LAMENTATION
WE TUMBLED TO THE GROUND...

NOTES

REVERSED

fear of change, lies, imprisonment
narrow avoidance of disaster

16

THE STAR

renewal

serenity

inspiration

hope

PAST SORROWS FADE,
THE FUTURE'S BRIGHT,
MOVE ON FROM STRUGGLE
INTO THE LIGHT ...

CARD 17 ✺ THE STAR ✺ NOTES ⁘ MAJOR ARCANA ⁘ XVII

REVERSED
DELAY
LACK OF SUCCESS, TIMING IS
NOT RIGHT, CONSIDER PAST
MISTAKES ...

18

THE

MOON

· ILLUSIONS · · FANTASIES · · DECEPTIONS ·
· THINGS MAY NOT BE AS THEY SEEM ·
· ANXIETY ·

MY LIGHT IS NOT SO CLEAR AS THE SUN'S RAYS
I MUTE THE SHAPE OF THINGS, IN MY SOFT GLOW
IT'S HARD TO TELL WHAT IS REAL
AND WHAT IMAGINING ...

NOTES

REVERSED
· PRIMAL FORCES AT WORK ·
· BLOCKED INTUITION OR CREATIVITY ·
· SAME AS UPRIGHT MEANINGS, BUT TO A
LESSER DEGREE ·

XIX

THE **Sun**

SUCCESS ☀ JOY ☀ WARMTH

☀ HAPPINESS

☀ RELATIONSHIPS ARE GOOD ☀

RADIANCE & JOY ARE MY GIFTS,
WARMTH FUELED BY THE PURE LIGHT OF HAPPINESS...

NOTES

REVERSED
FRUSTRATION
LACK OF SUCCESS
UNCLEAR
BLOCKS TO HAPPINESS

Judgement

XX · 20

○ rebirth ○ ○ renewal ○ ○ judgement ○

○ responsibility for actions ○

~ NOTES ~

THE TRUMPET SOUNDS
AND I ARISE
TO ANSWER FOR MY DOINGS,
AND HAVING DONE SO
I NOW PARTAKE
OF MY OWN RENEWING . . .

REVERSED
HAUNTED BY THE PAST, WEAK,
UNABLE TO LET GO, SELF-DOUBT, BLOCKED

THE WORLD

21   XXI

FULFILLMENT & SUCCESS   TRAVEL

COMPLETION OF CYCLE   LEARNING FROM LIFE LESSONS

FULFILLMENT & SUCCESS
OF MY OWN MAKING
THROUGH LESSONS LEARNED
AND JOURNEYS TAKEN . . .

NOTES

REVERSED
UNABLE TO COMPLETE PROJECTS
LACK OF CLOSURE   INERTIA

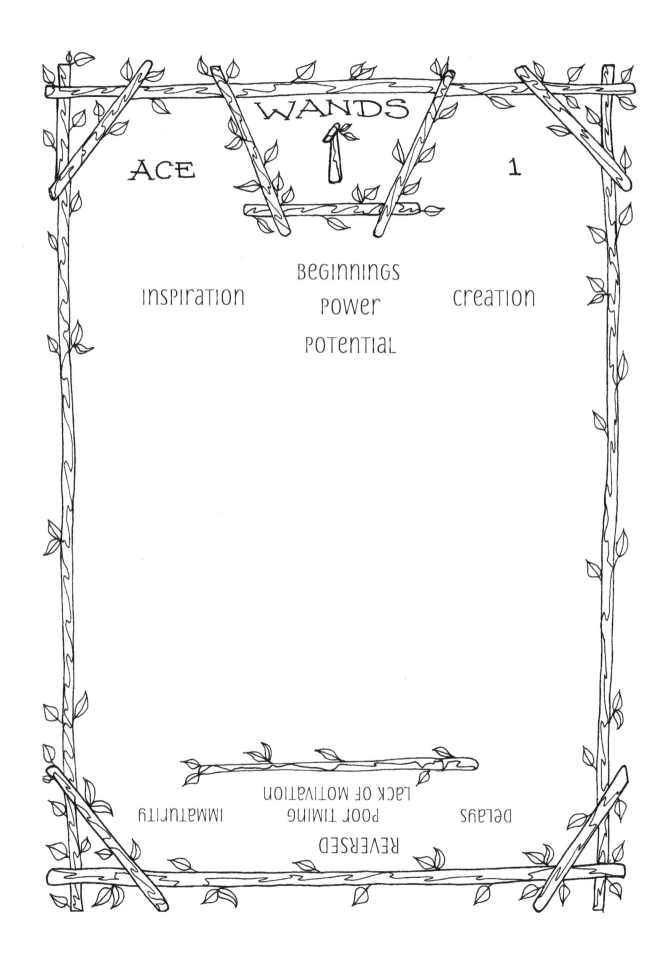

WANDS

ACE   1

INSPIRATION   BEGINNINGS   CREATION
                     POWER
                   POTENTIAL

REVERSED
IMMATURITY   POOR TIMING   DELAYS
              LACK OF MOTIVATION

WANDS

2

II   2

CONFIDENT   KNOWING WHAT YOU WANT

PROGRESS   DECISIONS   PLANNING FUTURE

LACK OF PLANNING   FEAR OF THE FUTURE
INDECISIVE   FEAR OF THE UNKNOWN

REVERSED

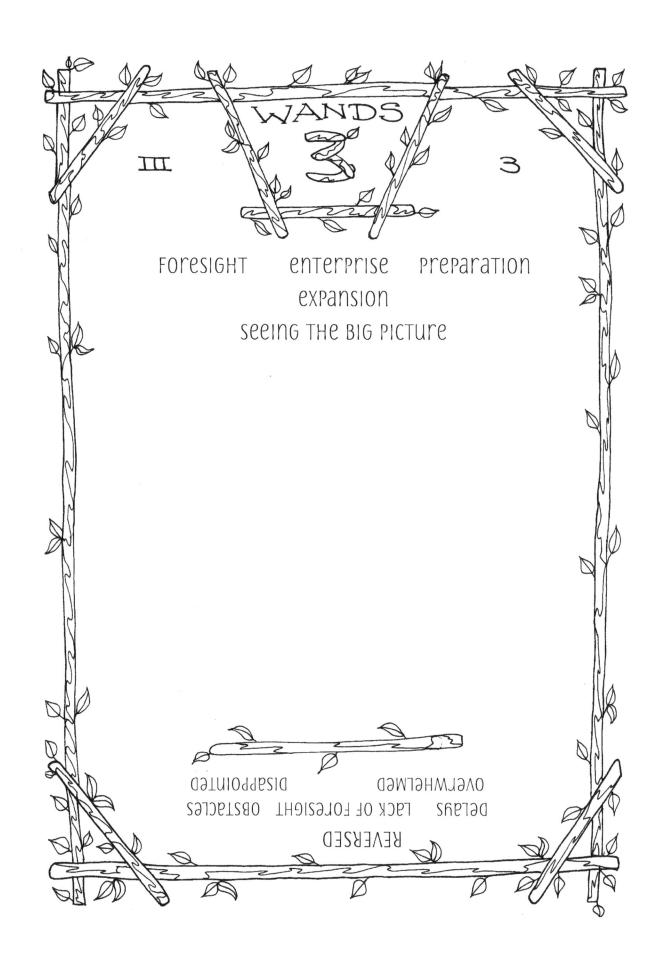

WANDS 3

III 3

FORESIGHT   ENTERPRISE   PREPARATION
EXPANSION
SEEING THE BIG PICTURE

REVERSED
DELAYS   LACK OF FORESIGHT   OBSTACLES
OVERWHELMED   DISAPPOINTED

WANDS

4

IV 4

HAPPY EVENT SUCH AS A MARRIAGE
CELEBRATION   COMMUNITY IN HARMONY
HOME LIFE   NEW POSSIBILITIES

REVERSED
CANCELLED EVENTS   TRANSITION
BREAKDOWN IN COMMUNICATION

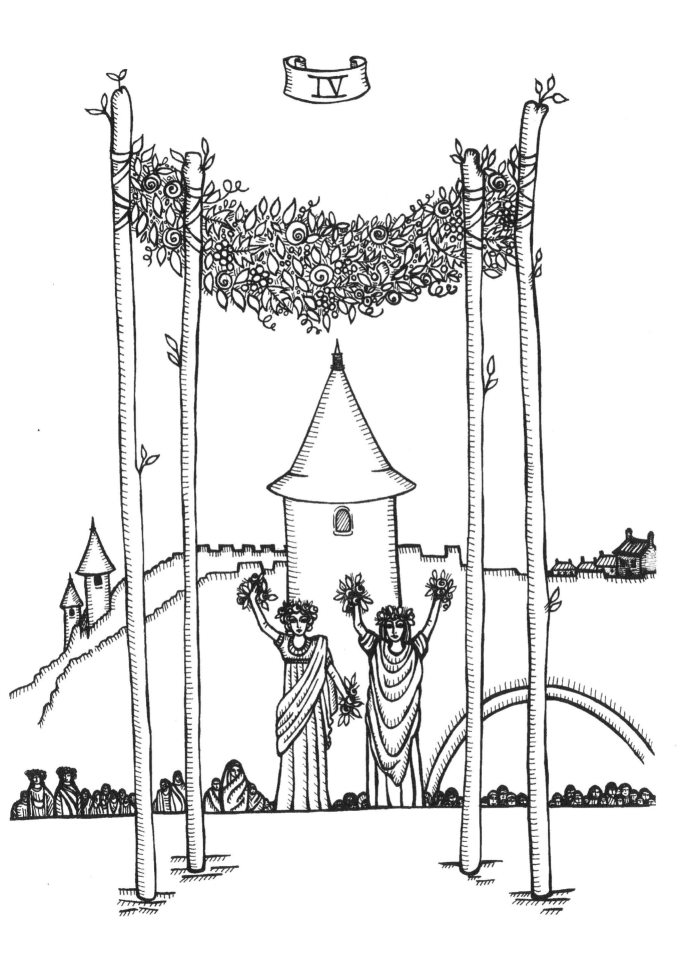

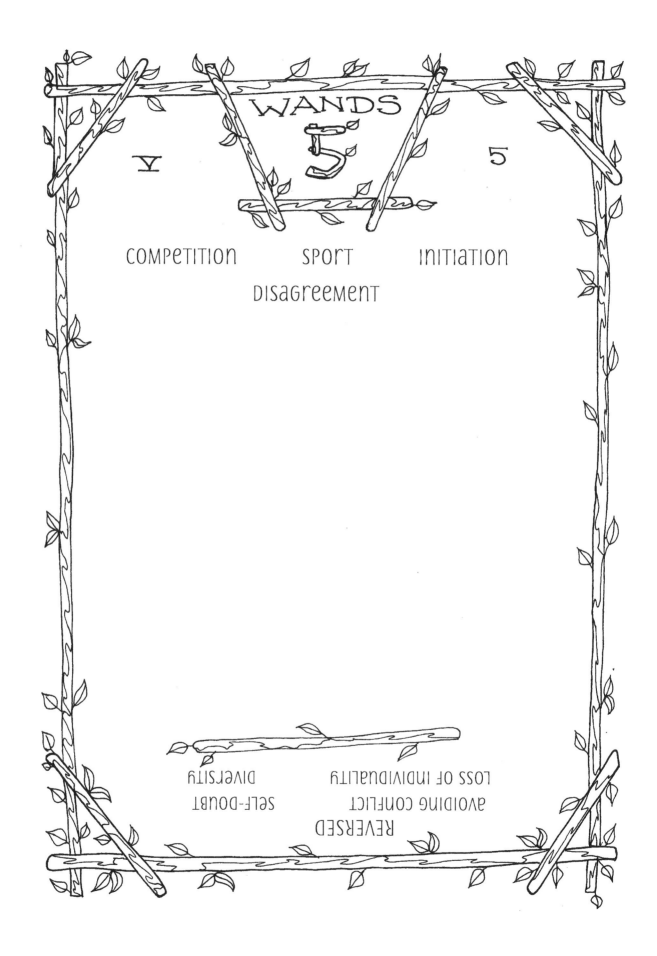

WANDS
5

Y   5

COMPETITION   SPORT   INITIATION

DISAGREEMENT

REVERSED
avoiding conflict   loss of individuality
self-doubt   diversity

WANDS

VI   6

PUBLIC RECOGNITION   VICTORY
GOOD FORTUNE   ELEVATION   SELF-CONFIDENCE

EGOTISM
FALL FROM GRACE   LACK OF CONFIDENCE   DEFEAT

REVERSED

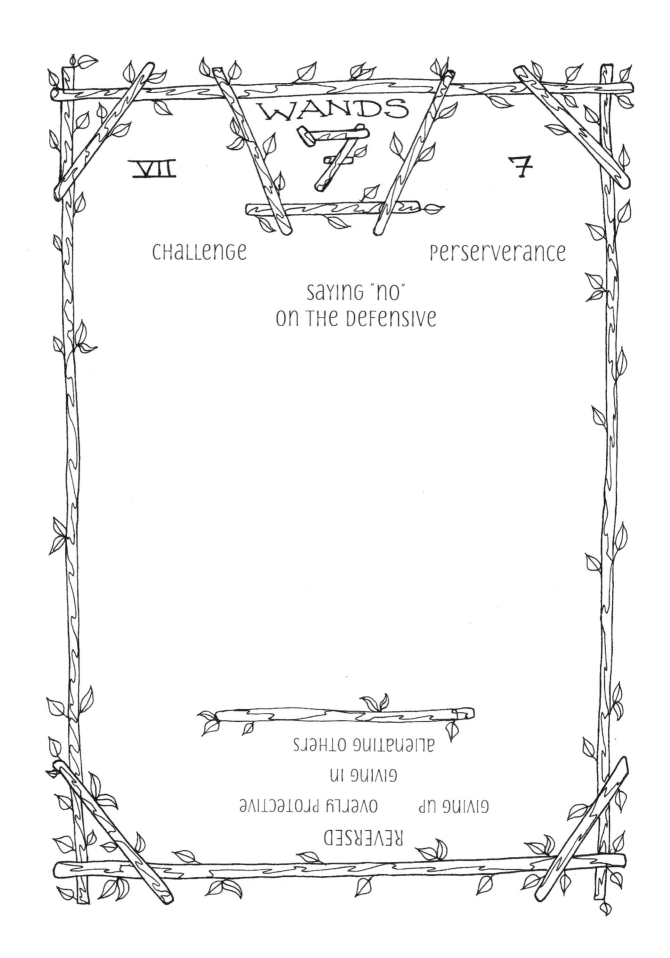

WANDS 7

VII   7

CHALLENGE   PERSERVERANCE

SAYING "NO"
ON THE DEFENSIVE

REVERSED

giving up   overly protective

giving in

alienating others

WANDS

VIII   8

SPEED   ACTION   SWIFT CHANGE

SWIFT MOVEMENT IN TRAVEL

REVERSED

WAITING   DISPUTES

FRUSTRATION   DELAYS

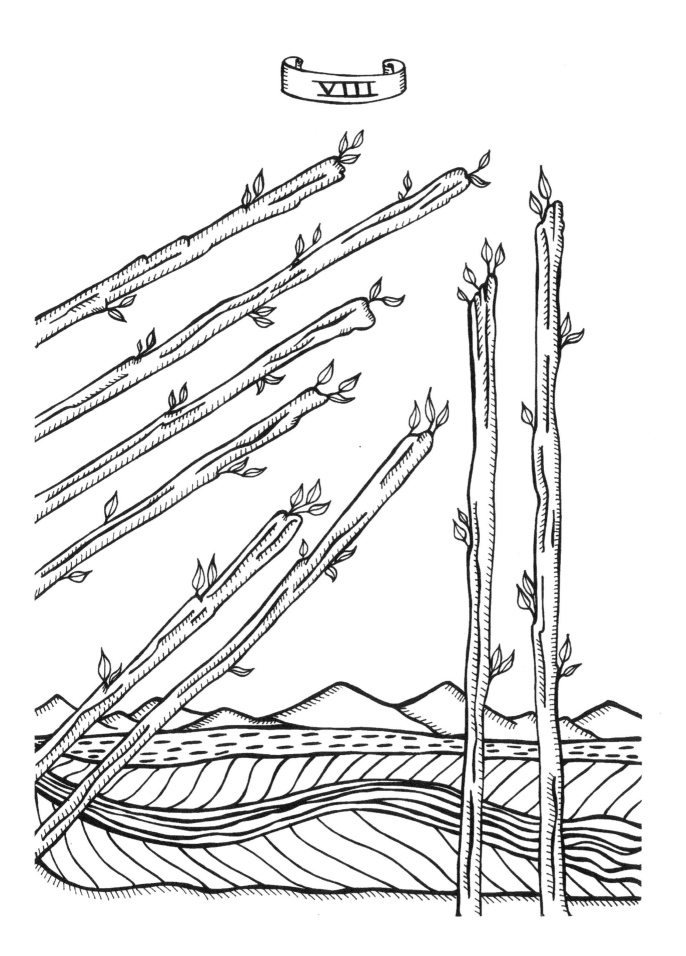

WANDS

IX   9

courage   resilience   persistence

STRONG BELIEFS = READY TO DEFEND

weak

suspicious   defensive

REVERSED

WANDS

X **10** **10**

HARD WORK   BURDEN   STRESS

RESPONSIBILITY   CAN'T SAY "NO"

"MARTYR"

REVERSED
TAKING ON TOO MUCH
BREAKING UNDER PRESSURE
AVOIDING RESPONSIBILITY

WANDS
PAGE

PERSON OF ENTHUSIASM   FREE SPIRIT

RISK TAKER   DISCOVERY   YOUTHFUL ENERGY

REVERSED

SETBACKS   PESSIMISM

BULLY

BAD NEWS

WANDS
KNIGHT

PERSON OF ENERGY & PASSION   ACTION

ADVENTURE   IMPULSIVE   SELF-CONFIDENT

REVERSED

HASTE   ADDICTION   FRUSTRATION

DELAYS   SCATTERED ENERGY   ARGUMENTS

KNIGHT

WANDS
QUEEN

PERSON OF EXUBERANCE & WARMTH

VIVACIOUS   DETERMINED

AMBITIOUS

DEMANDING   JEALOUS

AGGRESSIVE   TIMID

REVERSED

QUEEN

WANDS
KING

natural leader   entrepreneur

person of vision

someone ambitious & charismatic

REVERSED

high expectations   ruthless

impulsive   lazy   tyrannical

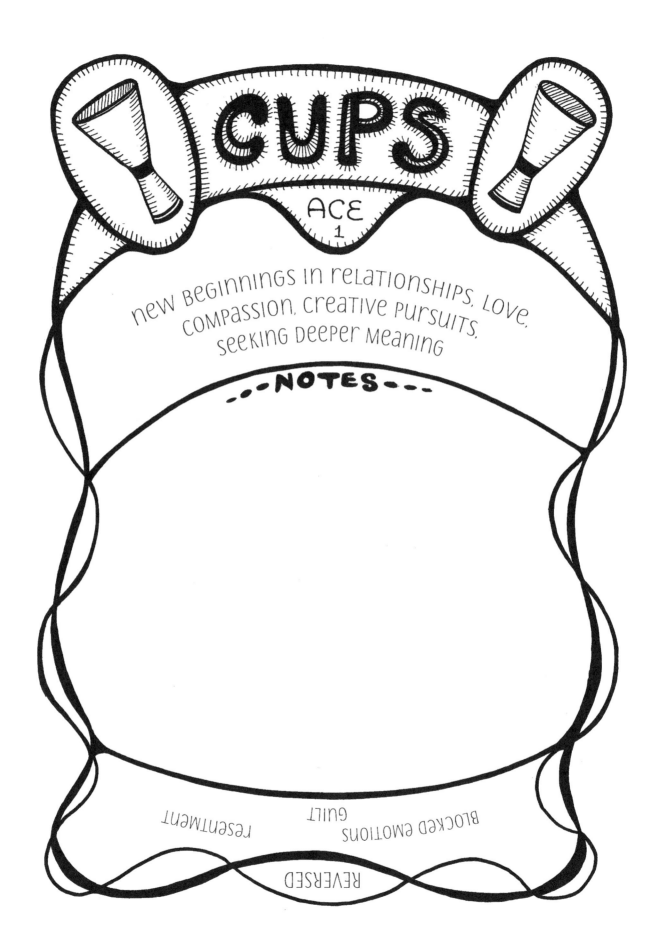

CUPS

ACE
1

new beginnings in relationships, love, compassion, creative pursuits, seeking deeper meaning

--- NOTES ---

REVERSED

BLOCKED EMOTIONS, GUILT, RESENTMENT

ACE of CUPS

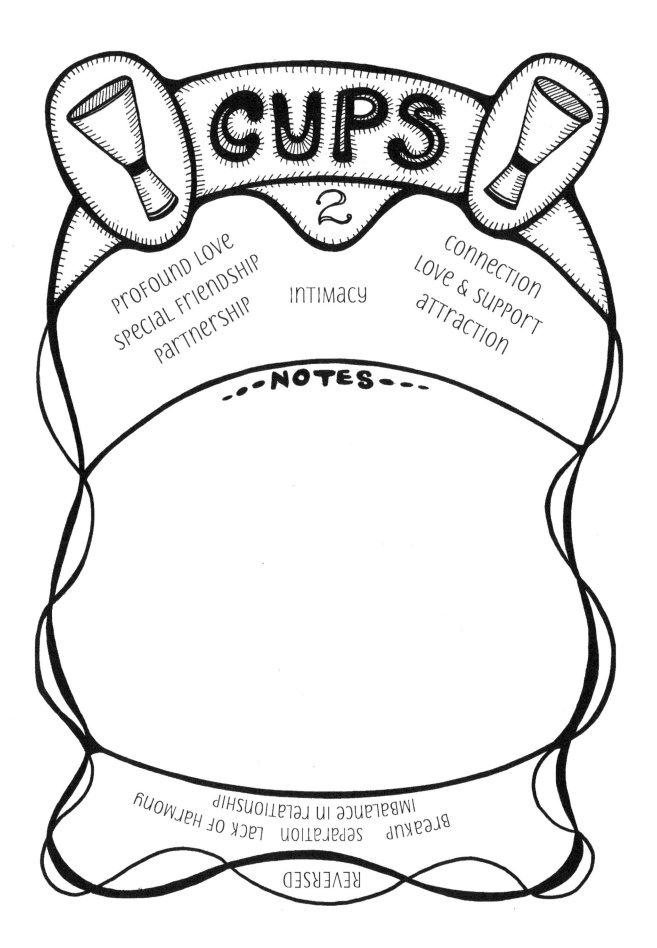

CUPS

2

PROFOUND LOVE
SPECIAL FRIENDSHIP
PARTNERSHIP

INTIMACY

CONNECTION
LOVE & SUPPORT
ATTRACTION

--·--NOTES--·--

REVERSED

BREAKUP SEPARATION LACK OF HARMONY
IMBALANCE IN RELATIONSHIP

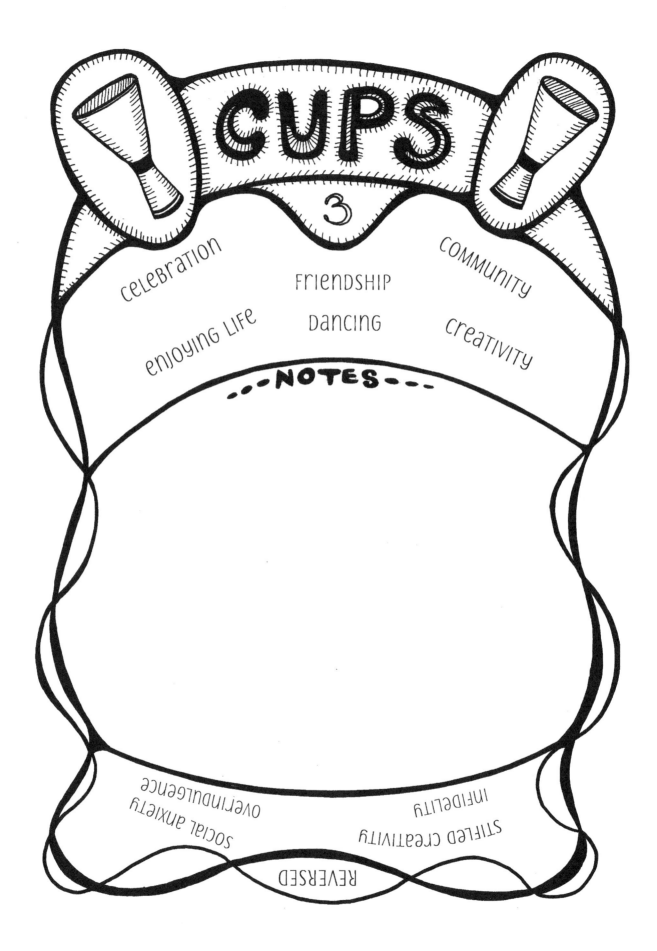

CUPS

3

CELEBRATION
FRIENDSHIP
COMMUNITY
ENJOYING LIFE
DANCING
CREATIVITY

- - - NOTES - - - -

social anxiety
overindulgence
INFIDELITY
STIFLED CREATIVITY

REVERSED

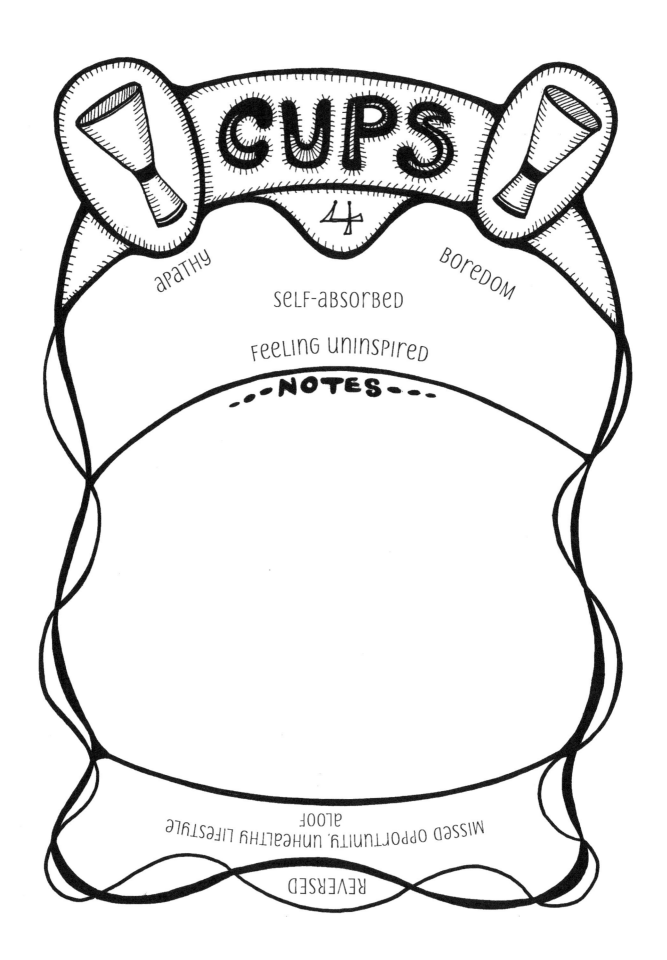

CUPS

4

APATHY

BOREDOM

SELF-ABSORBED

FEELING UNINSPIRED

---NOTES---

REVERSED

ALOOF

MISSED OPPORTUNITY UNHEALTHY LIFESTYLE

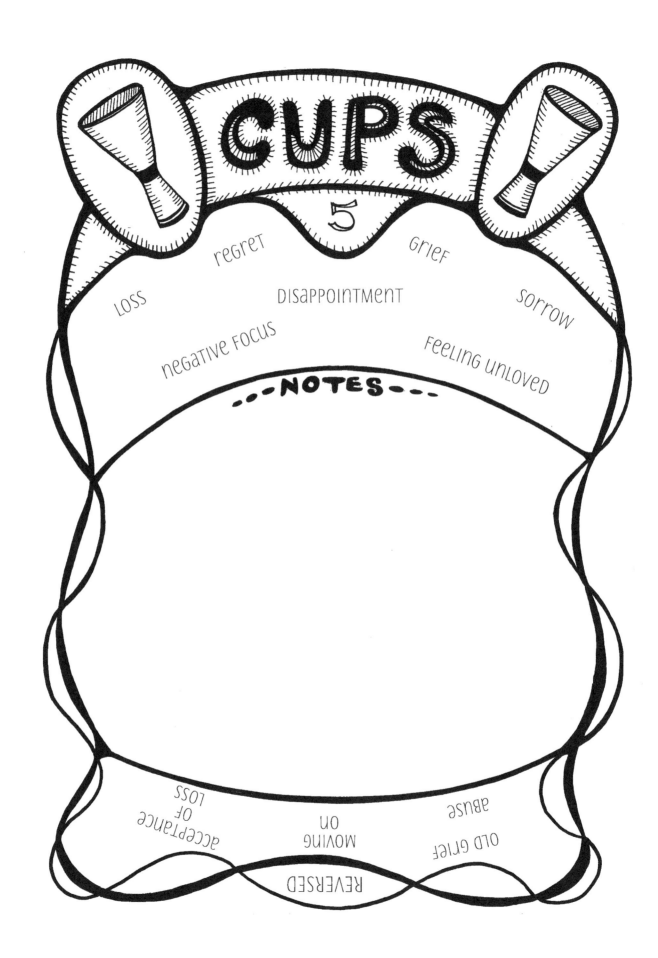

CUPS

5

REGRET   GRIEF

LOSS   DISAPPOINTMENT   SORROW

NEGATIVE FOCUS   FEELING UNLOVED

---NOTES---

ACCEPTANCE OF LOSS   MOVING ON   OLD GRIEF ABUSE

REVERSED

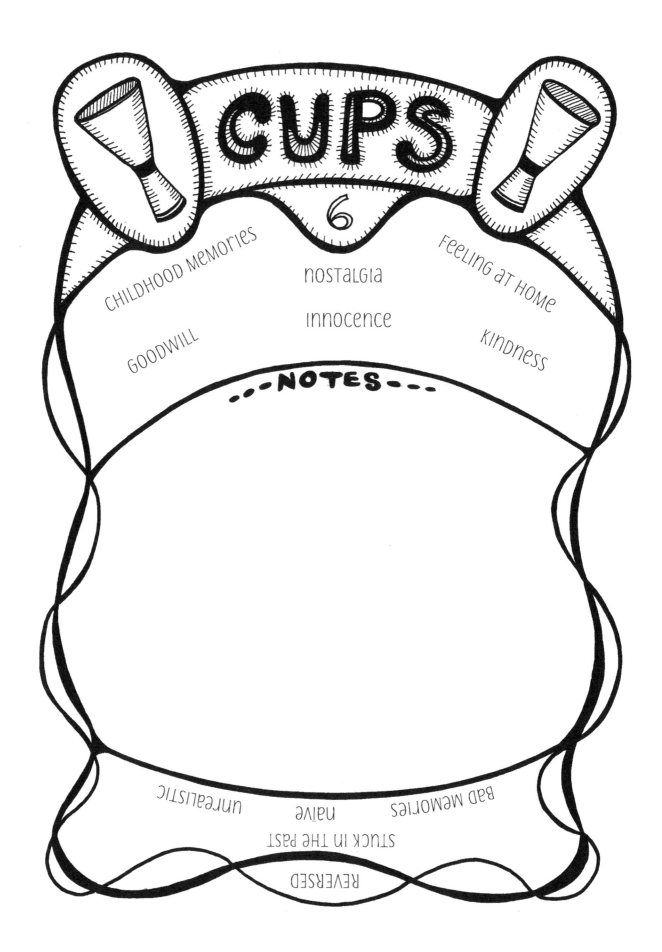

CUPS

6

CHILDHOOD MEMORIES   NOSTALGIA   FEELING AT HOME

GOODWILL   INNOCENCE   KINDNESS

---NOTES---

UNREALISTIC   NAÏVE   BAD MEMORIES

STUCK IN THE PAST

REVERSED

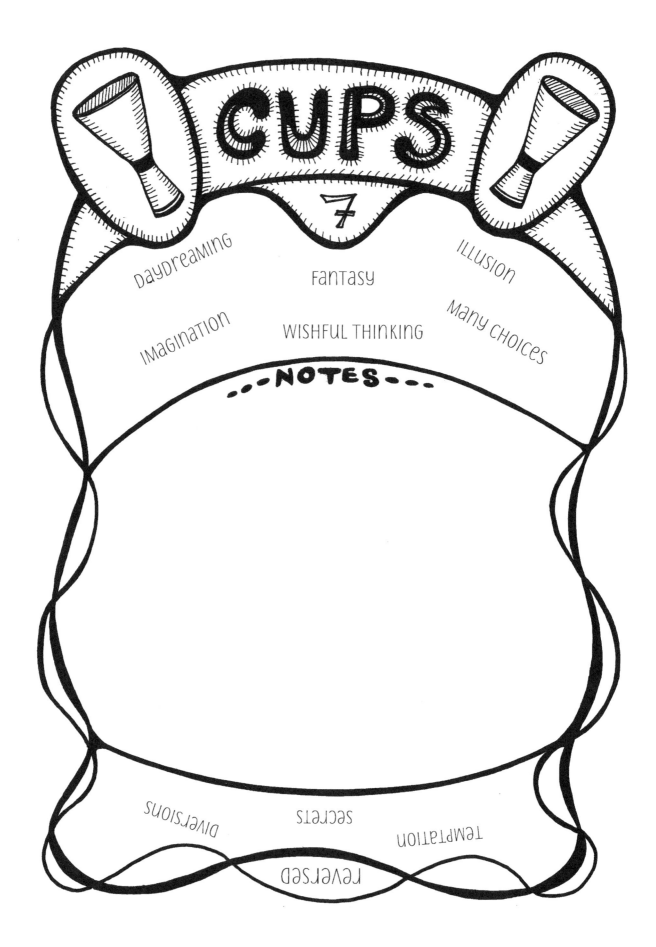

CUPS 7

DAYDREAMING

FANTASY

ILLUSION

IMAGINATION

WISHFUL THINKING

MANY CHOICES

---NOTES---

DIVERSIONS

SECRETS

TEMPTATION

REVERSED

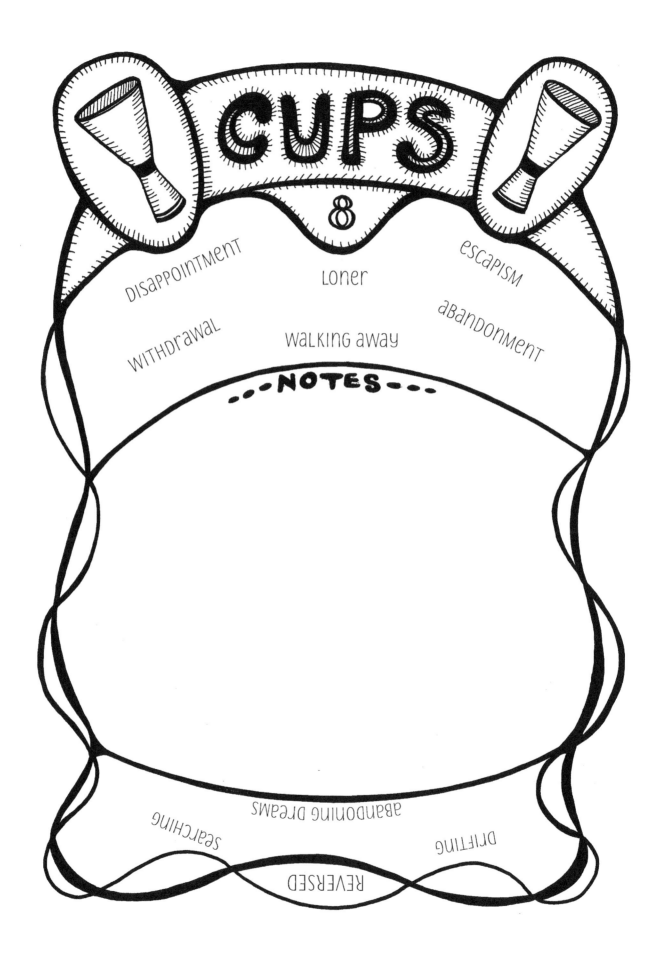

CUPS

8

DISAPPOINTMENT   LONER   ESCAPISM

ABANDONMENT

WITHDRAWAL   WALKING AWAY

···NOTES···

searching   abandoning dreams   drifting

REVERSED

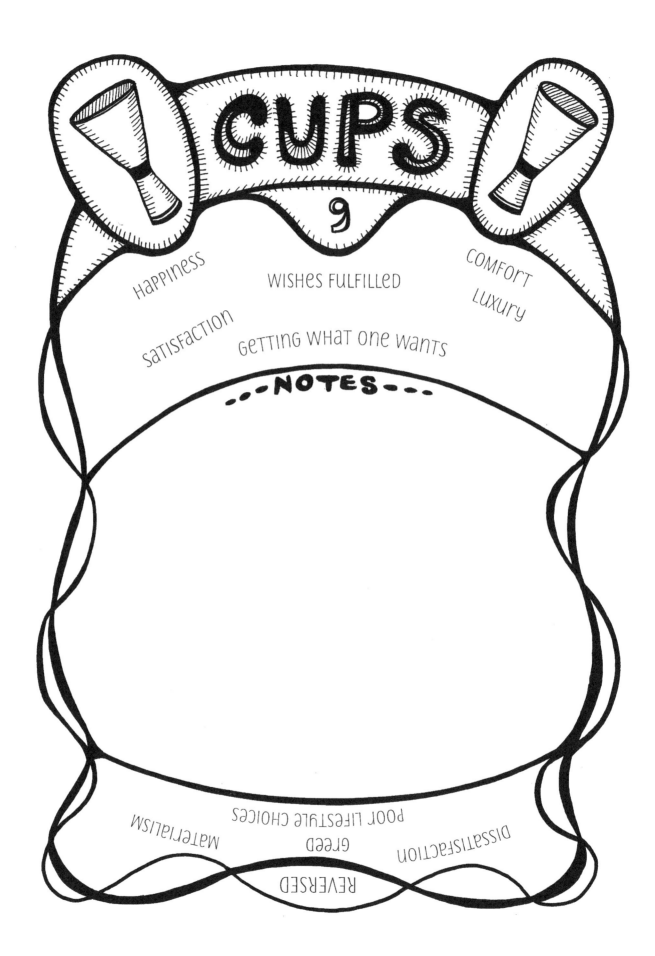

CUPS

9

Happiness
WISHES FULFILLED
COMFORT
Luxury
Satisfaction
GETTING WHAT ONE WANTS

---NOTES---

MATERIALISM
POOR LIFESTYLE CHOICES
GREED
DISSATISFACTION

REVERSED

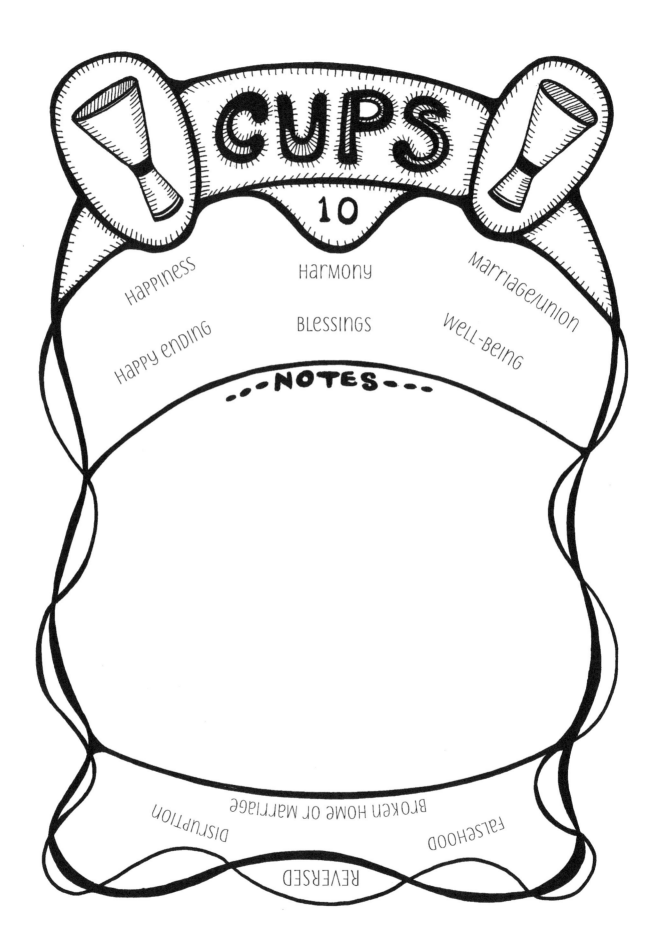

CUPS

10

HAPPINESS HARMONY MARRIAGE/UNION

HAPPY ENDING BLESSINGS WELL-BEING

---NOTES---

REVERSED

DISRUPTION BROKEN HOME OR MARRIAGE FALSEHOOD

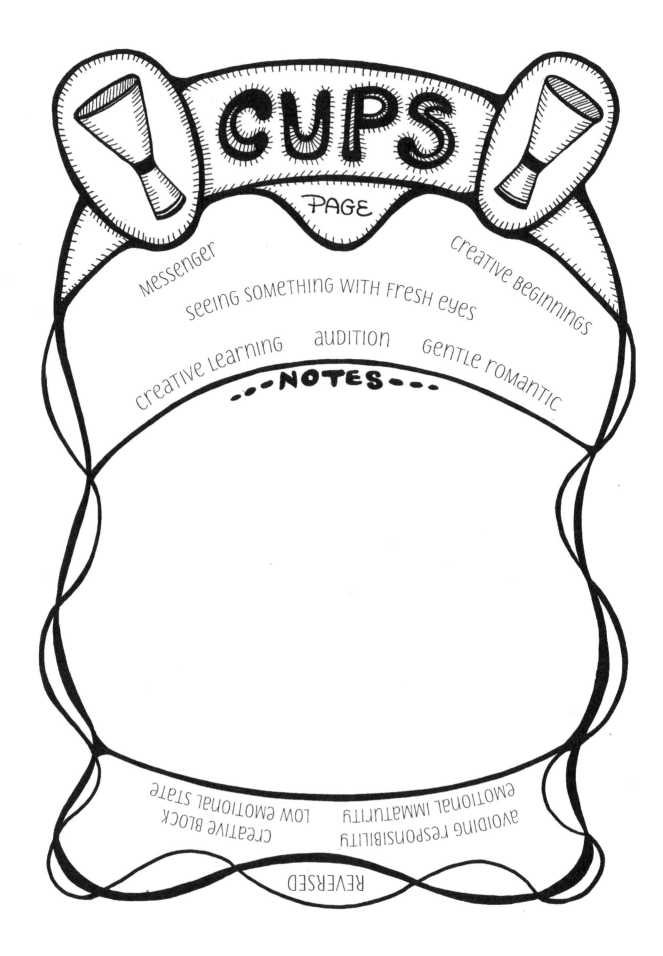

CUPS

PAGE

Messenger

SEEING SOMETHING WITH FRESH EYES

CREATIVE BEGINNINGS

CREATIVE LEARNING   AUDITION   GENTLE ROMANTIC

---NOTES---

REVERSED

CREATIVE BLOCK   LOW EMOTIONAL STATE   EMOTIONAL IMMATURITY   AVOIDING RESPONSIBILITY

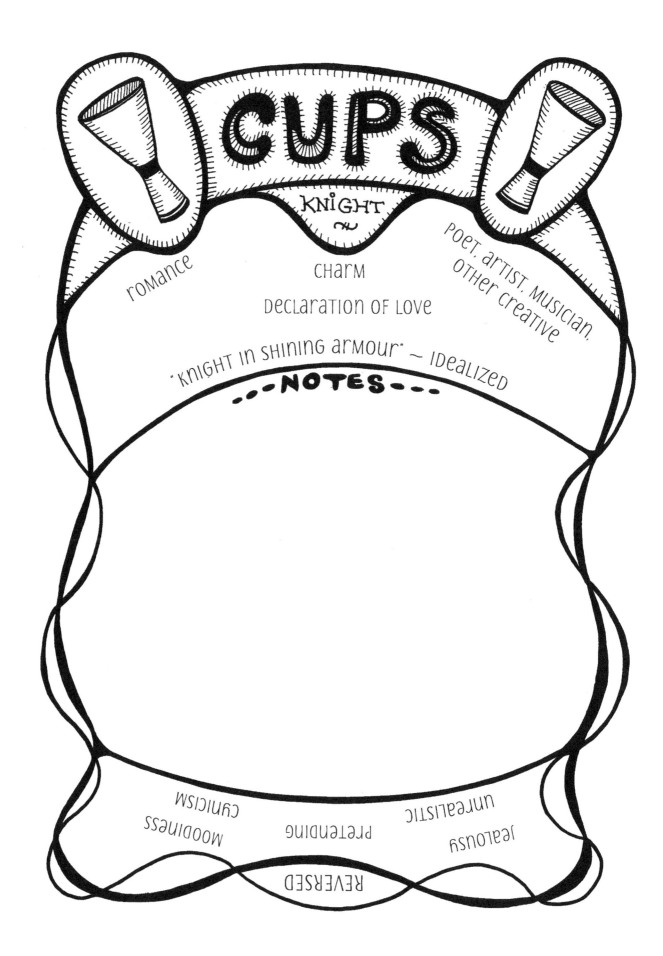

CUPS

KNIGHT

romance

charm

poet, artist, musician, other creative

declaration of love

"knight in shining armour" ~ idealized

---NOTES---

REVERSED

moodiness

cynicism

pretending

unrealistic

jealousy

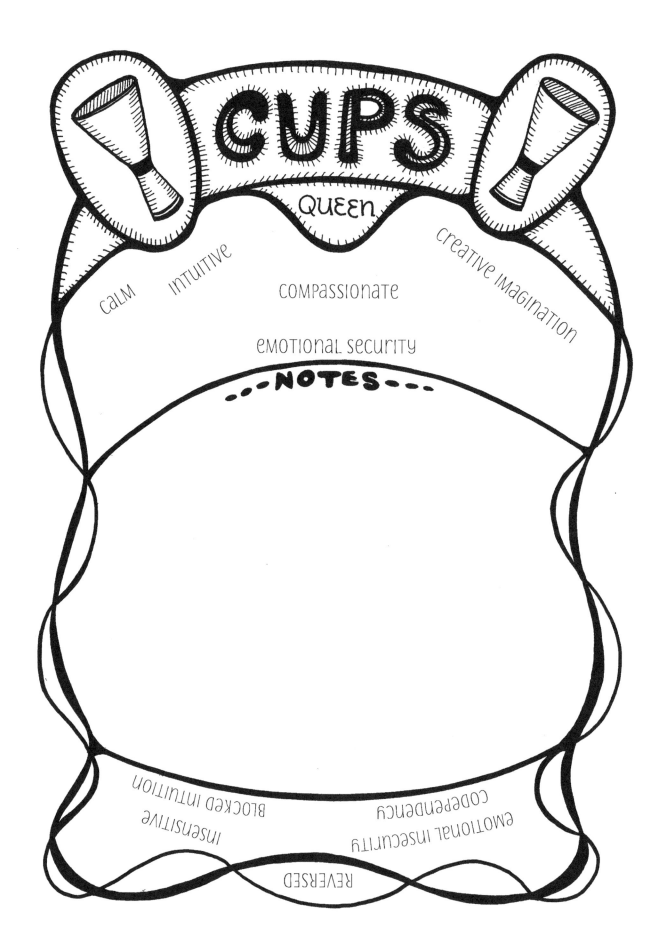

CUPS

QUEEN

CALM   INTUITIVE   COMPASSIONATE   CREATIVE IMAGINATION

EMOTIONAL SECURITY

...NOTES...

REVERSED

INSENSITIVE   BLOCKED INTUITION   EMOTIONAL INSECURITY   CODEPENDENCY

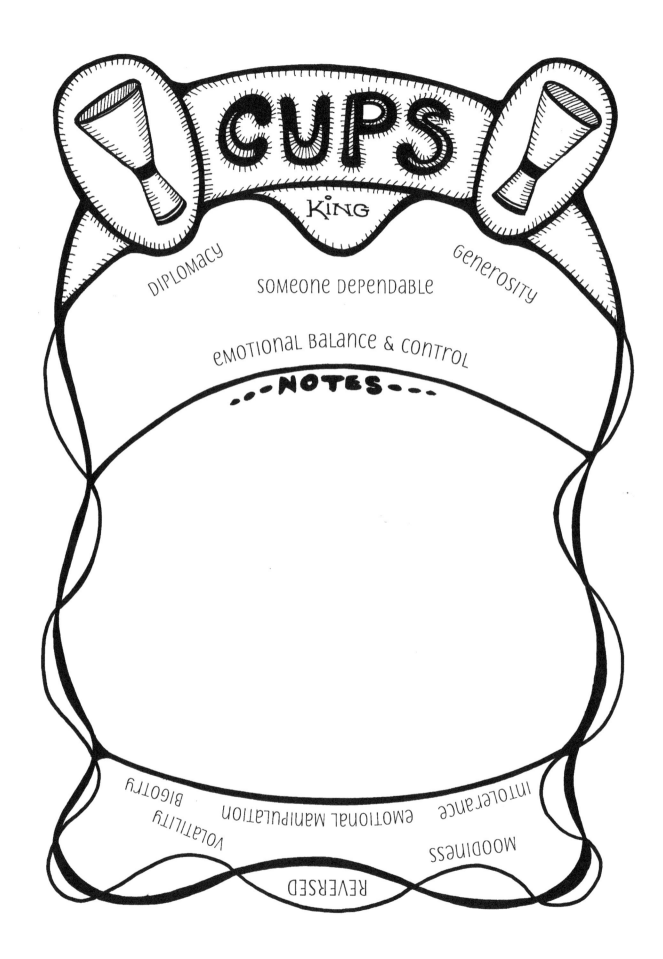

CUPS

KING

DIPLOMACY

SOMEONE DEPENDABLE

GENEROSITY

EMOTIONAL BALANCE & CONTROL

---NOTES---

BIGOTRY

VOLATILITY

EMOTIONAL MANIPULATION

INTOLERANCE

MOODINESS

REVERSED

KING

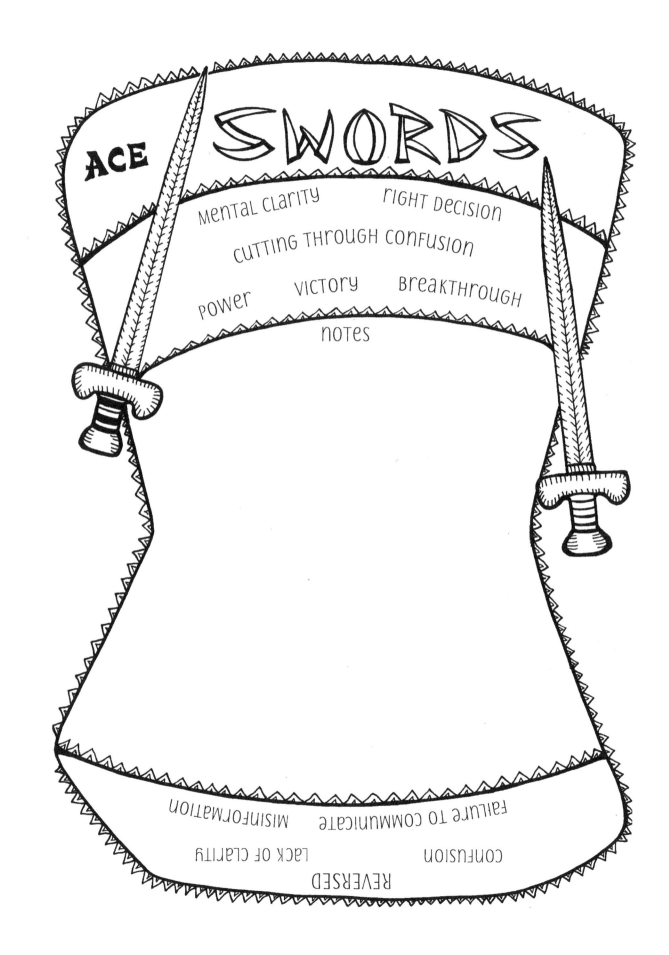

ACE SWORDS

MENTAL CLARITY   RIGHT DECISION

CUTTING THROUGH CONFUSION

POWER   VICTORY   BREAKTHROUGH

NOTES

REVERSED

confusion   LACK OF CLARITY

FAILURE TO COMMUNICATE   MISINFORMATION

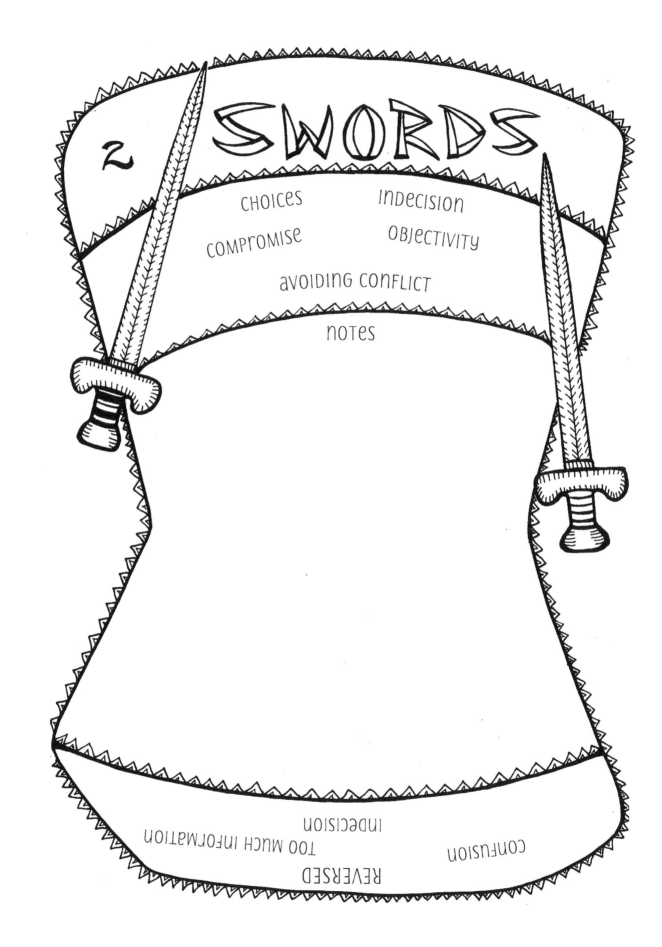

2 SWORDS

CHOICES   INDECISION

COMPROMISE   OBJECTIVITY

AVOIDING CONFLICT

NOTES

REVERSED
TOO MUCH INFORMATION
INDECISION
CONFUSION

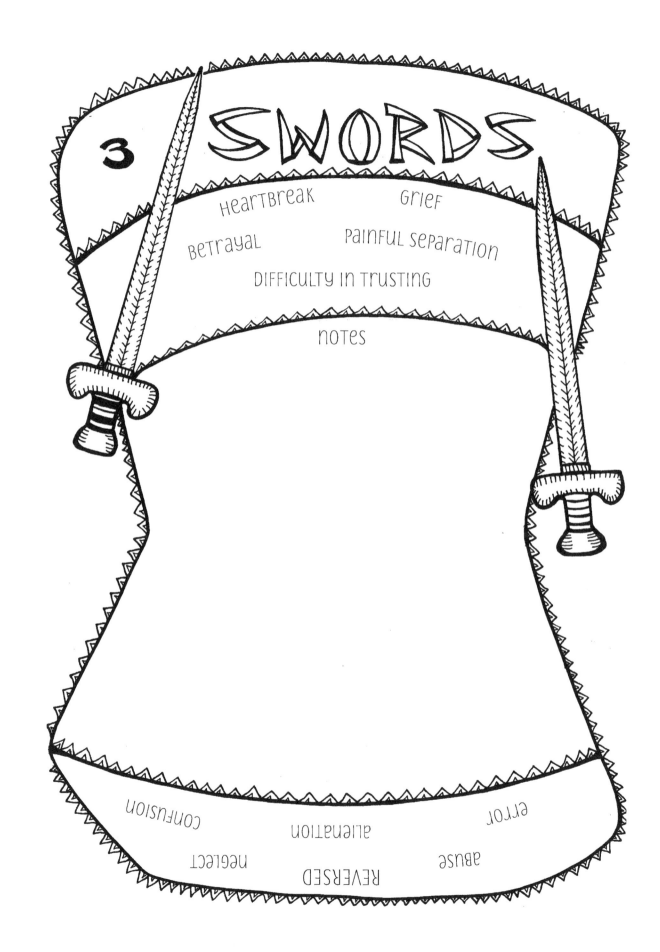

3 SWORDS

HEARTBREAK   GRIEF

BETRAYAL   PAINFUL SEPARATION

DIFFICULTY IN TRUSTING

NOTES

REVERSED

confusion   neglect   alienation   abuse   error

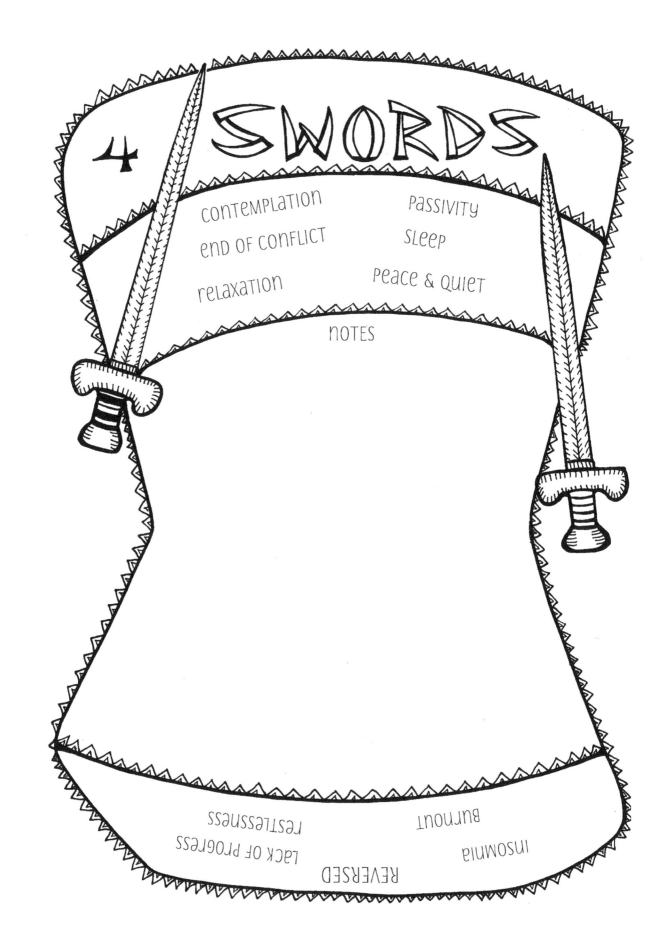

4 SWORDS

CONTEMPLATION   PASSIVITY
END OF CONFLICT   SLEEP

RELAXATION   PEACE & QUIET

NOTES

RESTLESSNESS   BURNOUT
LACK OF PROGRESS   INSOMNIA
REVERSED

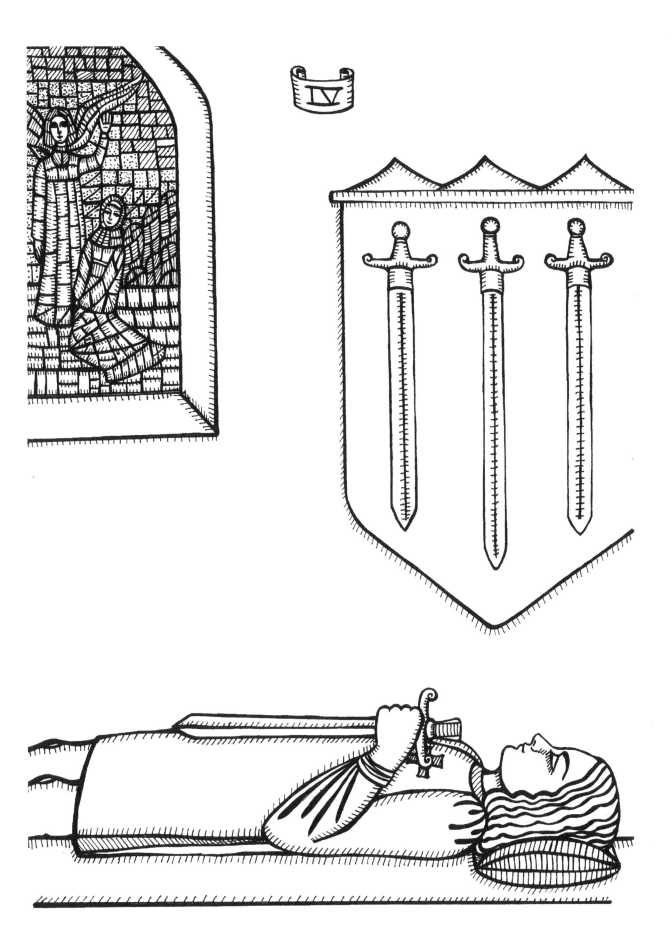

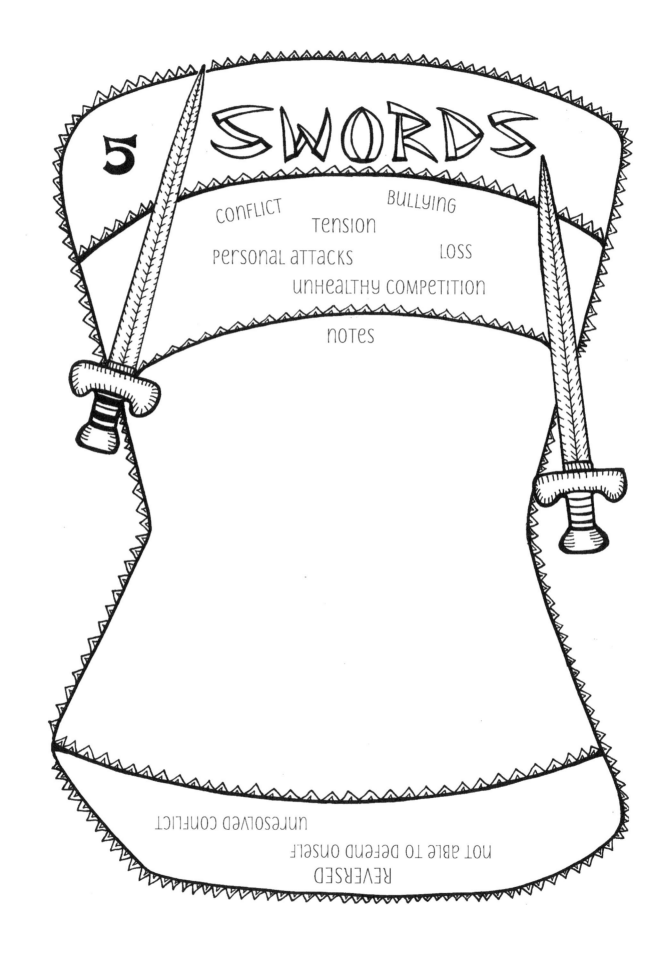

5

SWORDS

CONFLICT BULLYING

TENSION

PERSONAL ATTACKS LOSS

UNHEALTHY COMPETITION

NOTES

REVERSED
NOT ABLE TO DEFEND ONESELF
UNRESOLVED CONFLICT

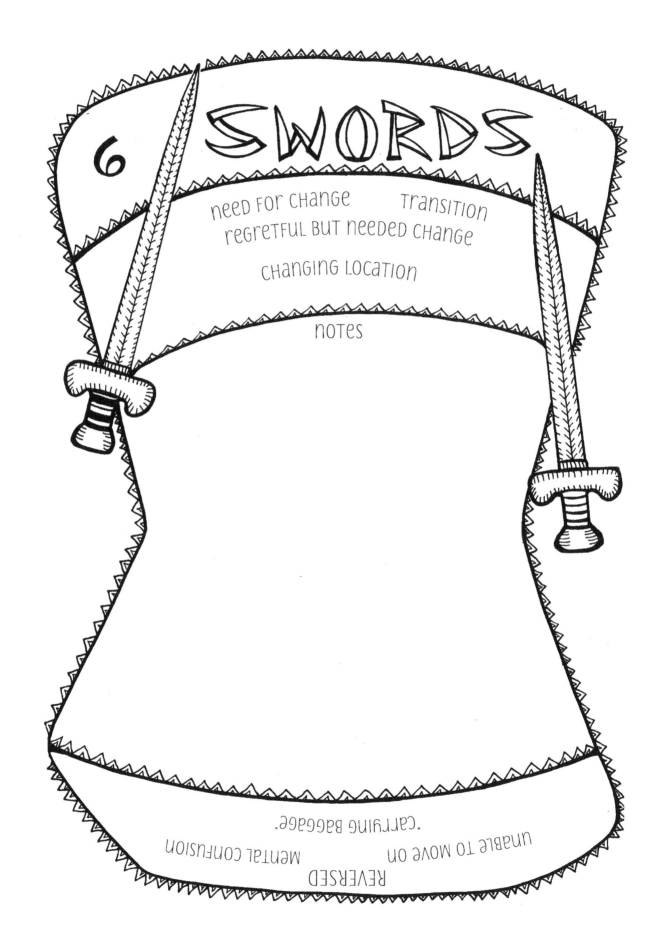

6 SWORDS

NEED FOR CHANGE   TRANSITION

REGRETFUL BUT NEEDED CHANGE

CHANGING LOCATION

NOTES

REVERSED

MENTAL CONFUSION   UNABLE TO MOVE ON

"CARRYING BAGGAGE."

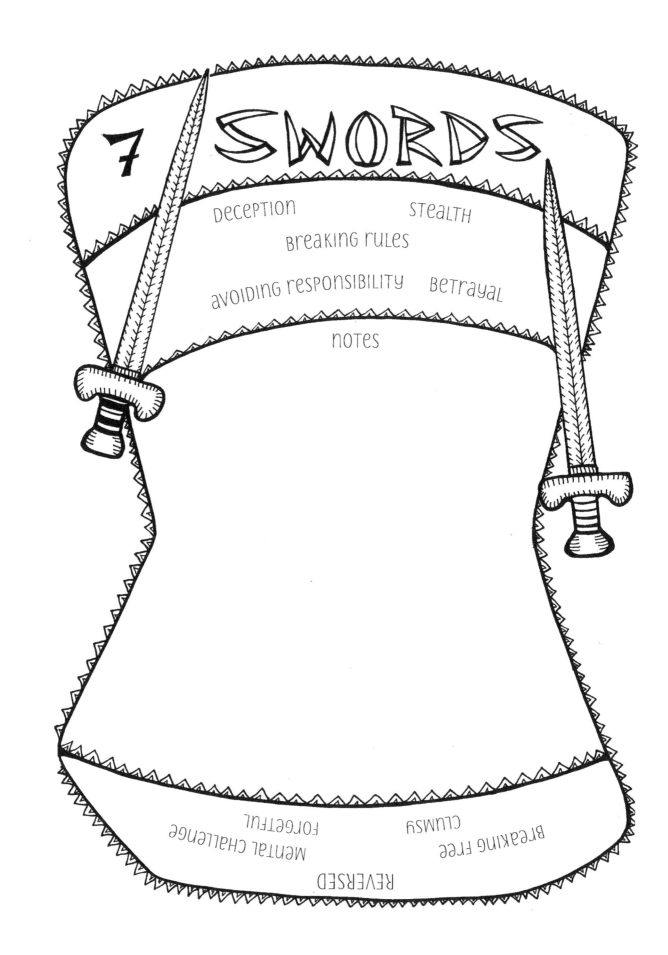

7 SWORDS

DECEPTION   STEALTH

BREAKING RULES

AVOIDING RESPONSIBILITY   BETRAYAL

NOTES

REVERSED

MENTAL CHALLENGE   CLUMSY
FORGETFUL   BREAKING FREE

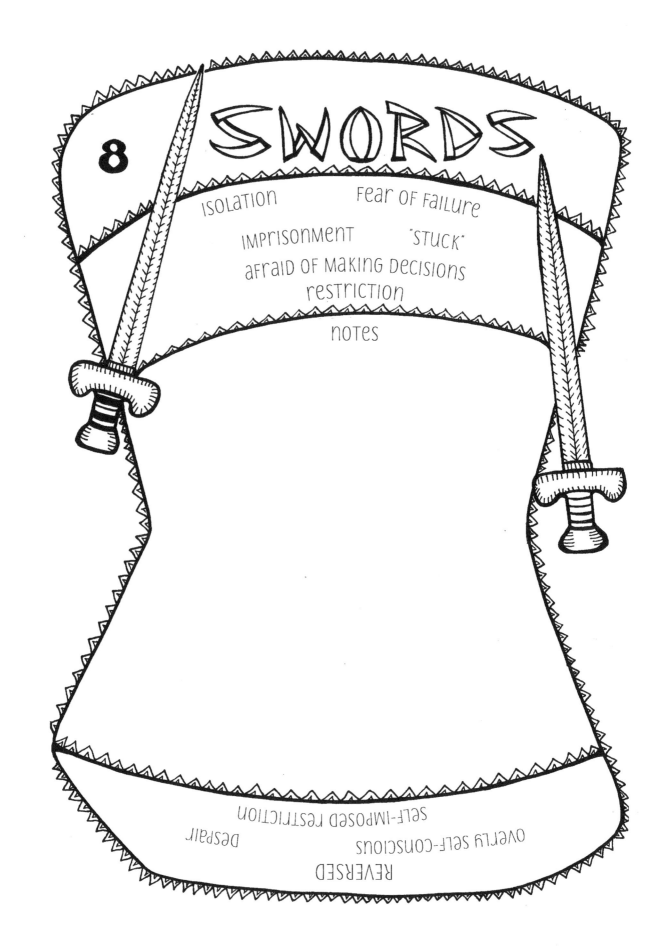

8

SWORDS

ISOLATION   Fear OF Failure

IMPRISONMENT   "STUCK"

afraid OF making Decisions

restriction

notes

REVERSED

Despair   overly self-conscious   self-imposed restriction

9 SWORDS

DEPRESSION

NIGHTMARES

DECEPTION

INTENSE ANXIETY

EXTREME NEGATIVITY

FEELING UNWORTHY

NOTES

REVERSED

extreme DEPRESSION

TORMENT

DESPAIR

HOPELESSNESS

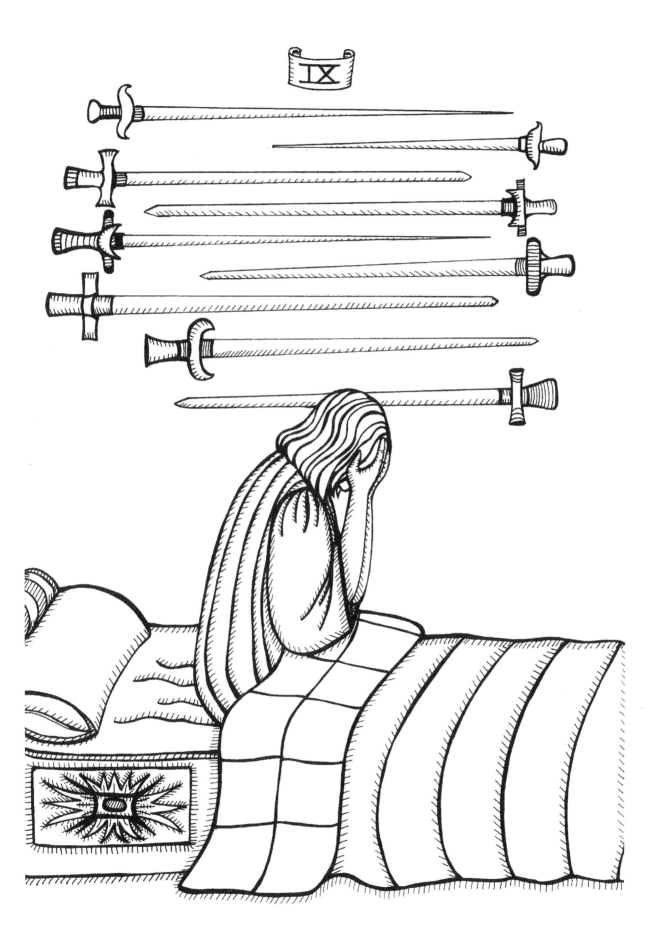

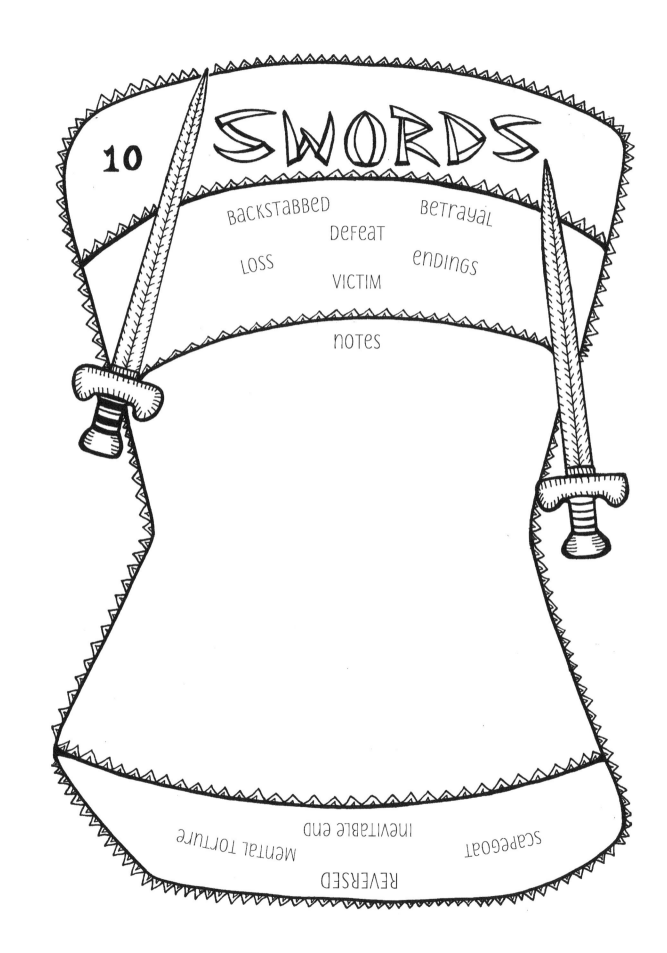

10

SWORDS

BACKSTABBED   BETRAYAL

DEFEAT

LOSS   ENDINGS

VICTIM

NOTES

REVERSED

Mental torture   inevitable end   scapegoat

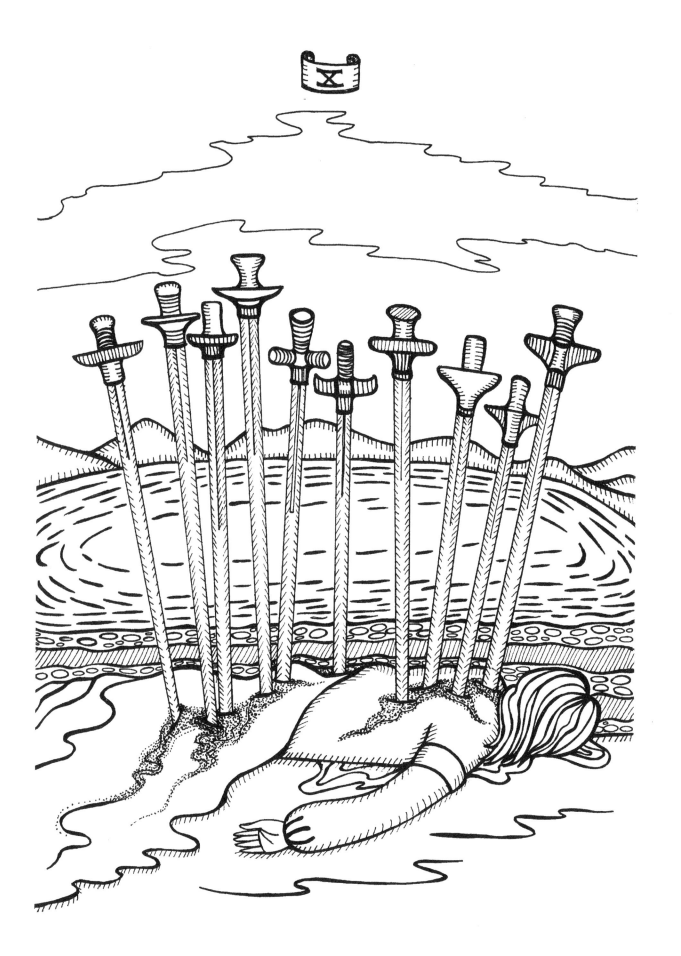

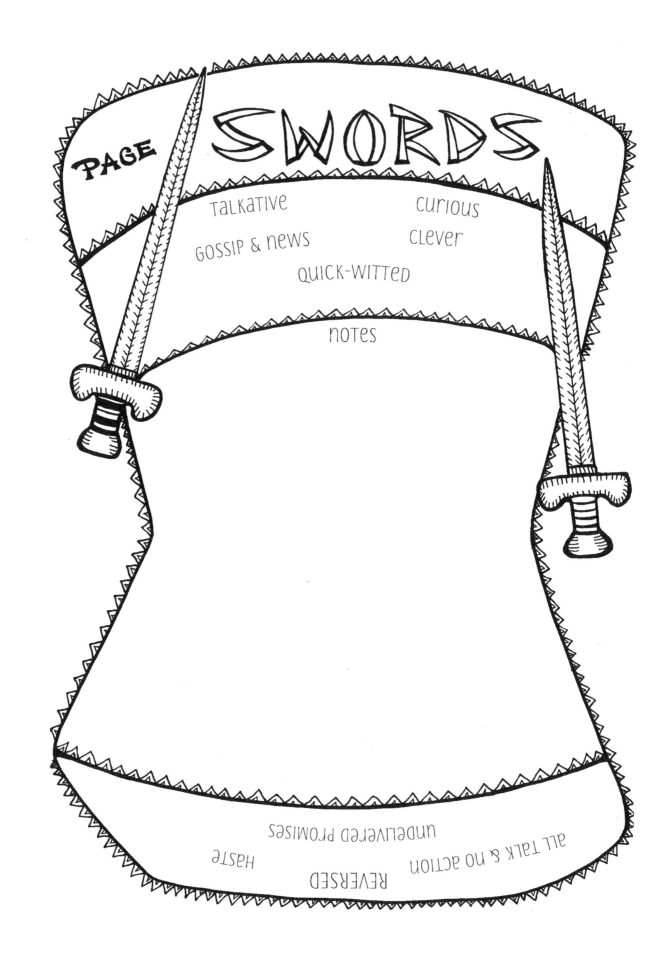

PAGE **SWORDS**

TALKATIVE   CURIOUS

GOSSIP & NEWS   CLEVER

QUICK-WITTED

NOTES

UNDELIVERED PROMISES

HASTE

REVERSED   ALL TALK & NO ACTION

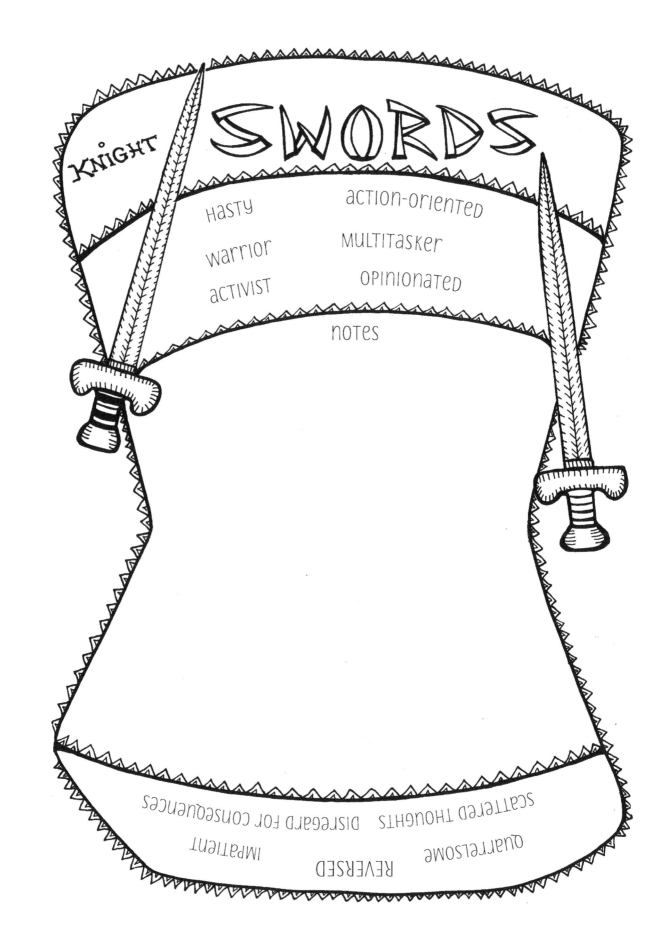

Knight

SWORDS

HASTY

action-oriented

warrior

MULTITASKER

ACTIVIST

OPINIONATED

notes

REVERSED

scattered thoughts   disregard for consequences

impatient   quarrelsome

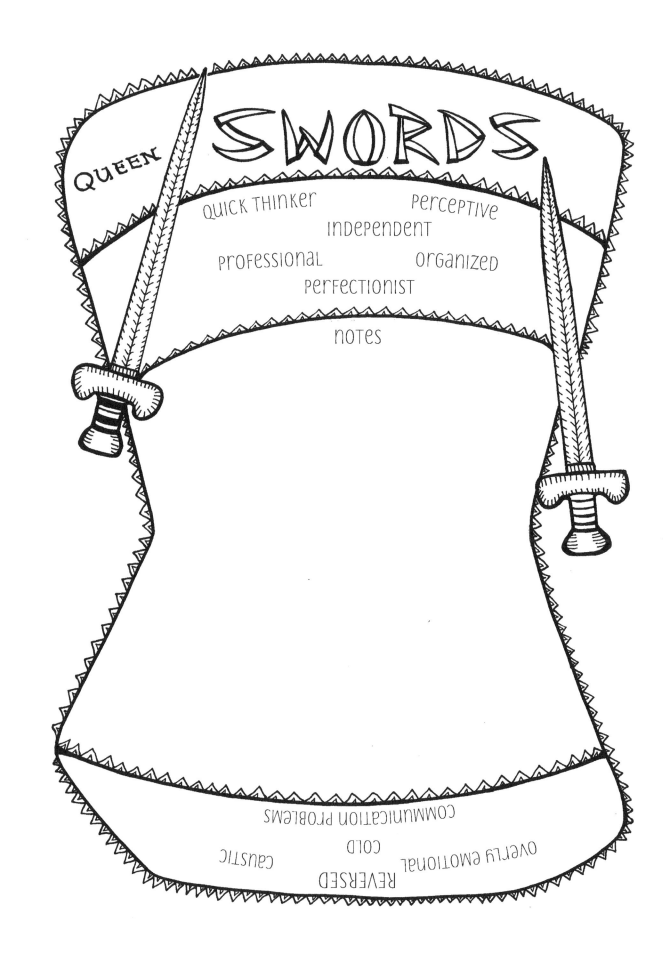

QUEEN SWORDS

QUICK THINKER   PERCEPTIVE

INDEPENDENT

PROFESSIONAL   ORGANIZED

PERFECTIONIST

NOTES

COMMUNICATION PROBLEMS

COLD

REVERSED   OVERLY EMOTIONAL

CAUSTIC

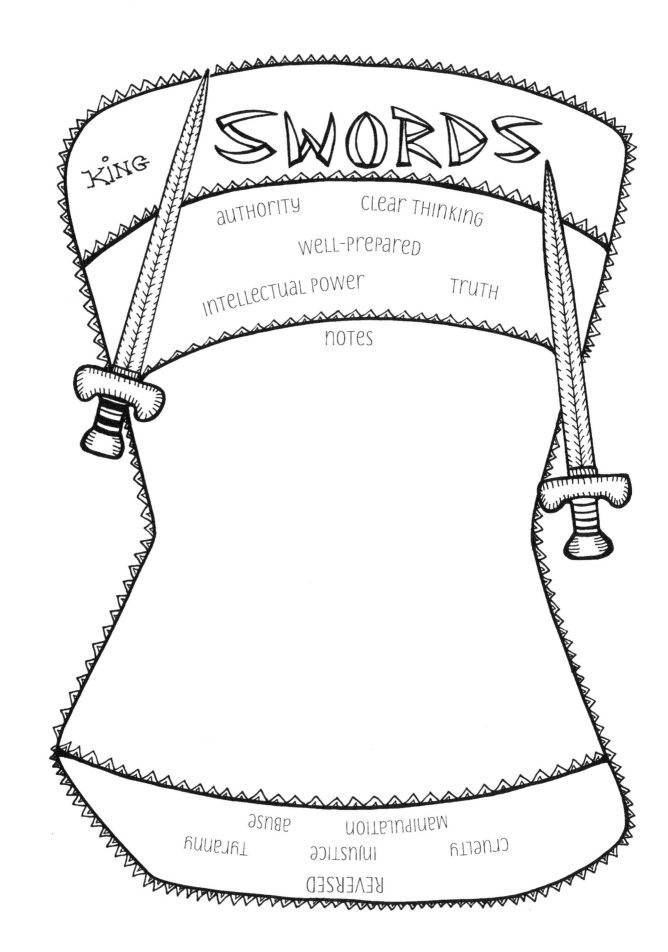

KING SWORDS

AUTHORITY   CLEAR THINKING

WELL-PREPARED

INTELLECTUAL POWER   TRUTH

NOTES

REVERSED

TYRANNY   INJUSTICE   MANIPULATION   CRUELTY   ABUSE

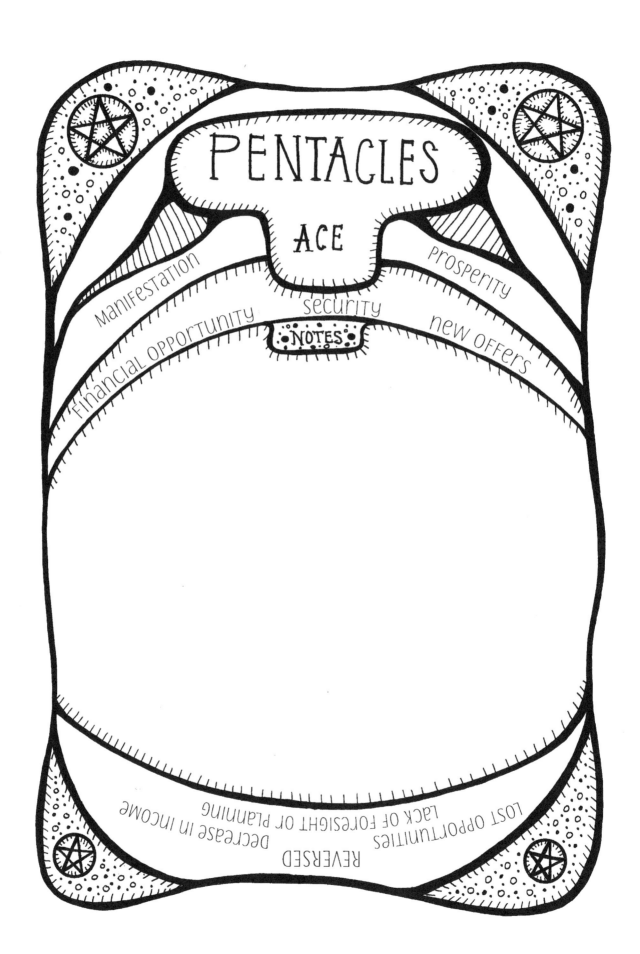

ACE of PENTACLES

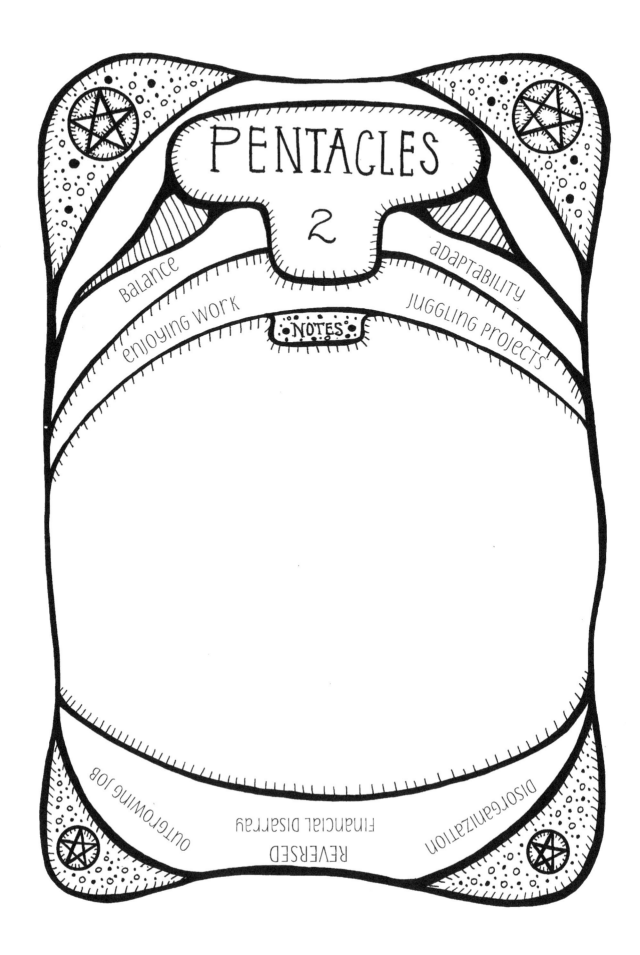

PENTACLES

2

Balance

adaptability

enjoying work

JUGGLING PROJECTS

NOTES

outgrowing job

REVERSED
Financial Disarray

Disorganization

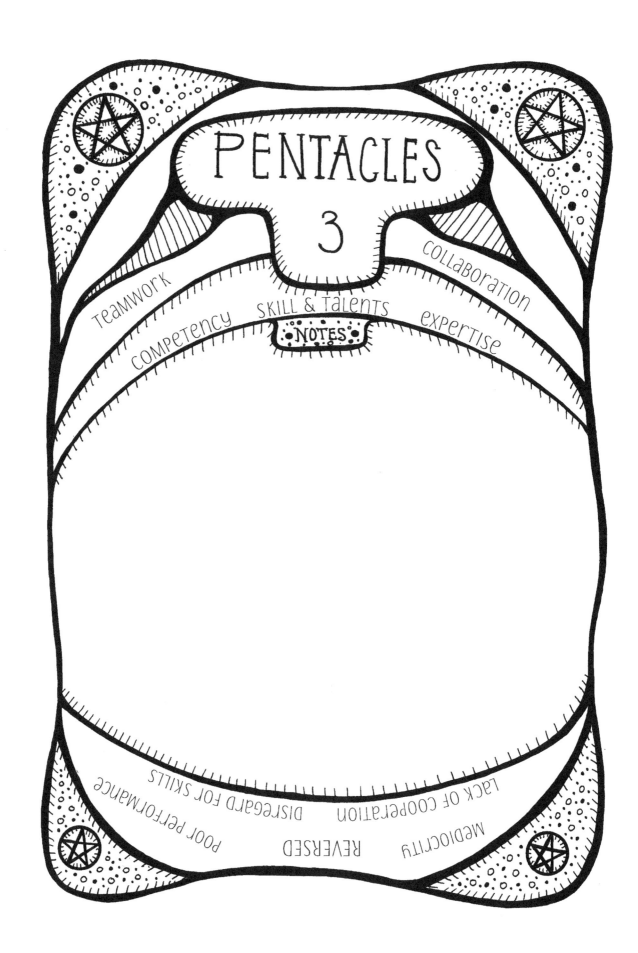

PENTACLES

3

Teamwork
COLLABORATION
COMPETENCY
SKILL & TALENTS
NOTES
EXPERTISE

LACK OF SKILLS
DISREGARD FOR SKILLS
LACK OF COOPERATION
POOR PERFORMANCE
REVERSED
MEDIOCRITY

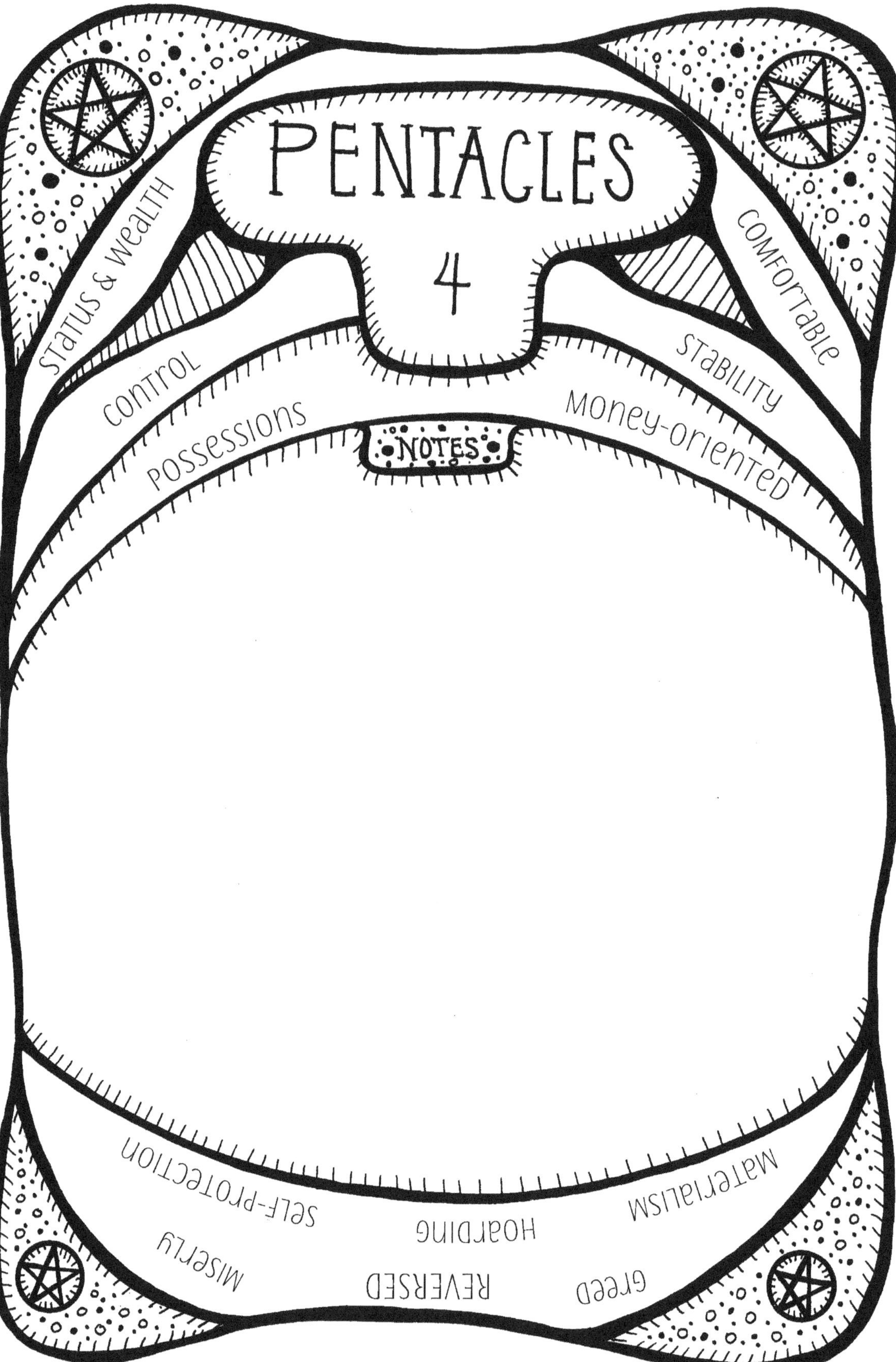

PENTACLES

4

STATUS & WEALTH

COMFORTABLE

CONTROL

STABILITY

POSSESSIONS

MONEY-ORIENTED

NOTES

MATERIALISM

SELF-PROTECTION

HOARDING

MISERLY

REVERSED

GREED

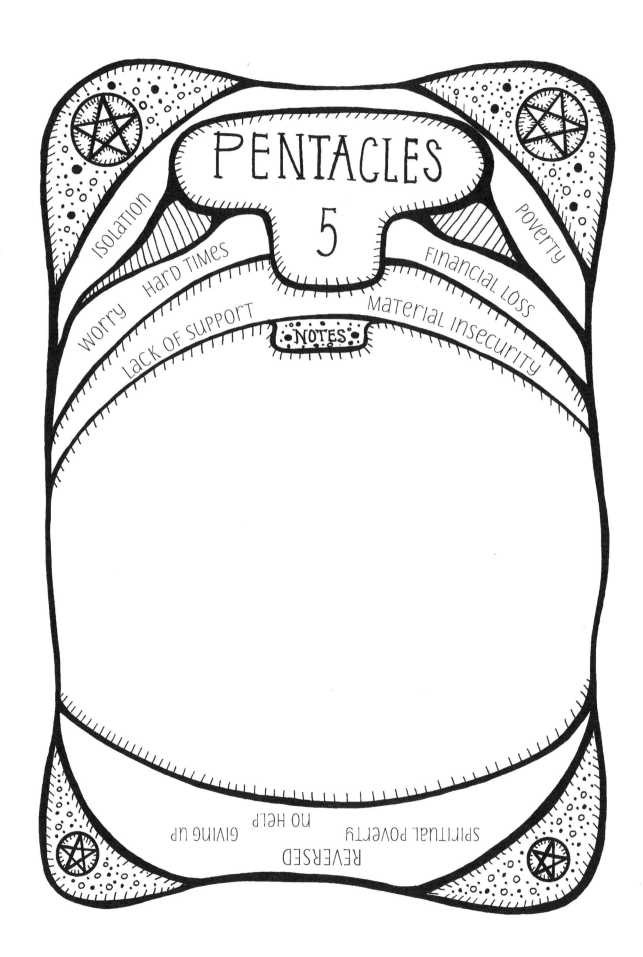

PENTACLES
5

ISOLATION

POVERTY

HARD TIMES

FINANCIAL LOSS

WORRY

LACK OF SUPPORT

MATERIAL INSECURITY

NOTES

REVERSED

SPIRITUAL POVERTY   NO HELP

GIVING UP

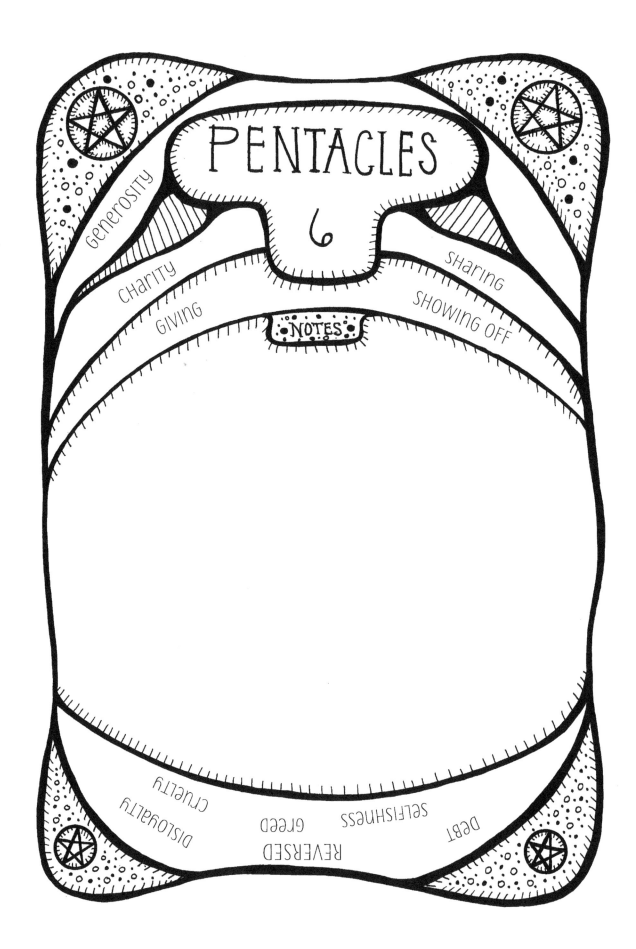

PENTACLES

6

Generosity

Charity

Giving

Sharing

SHOWING OFF

NOTES

REVERSED

DISLOYALTY

CRUELTY

GREED

SELFISHNESS

DEBT

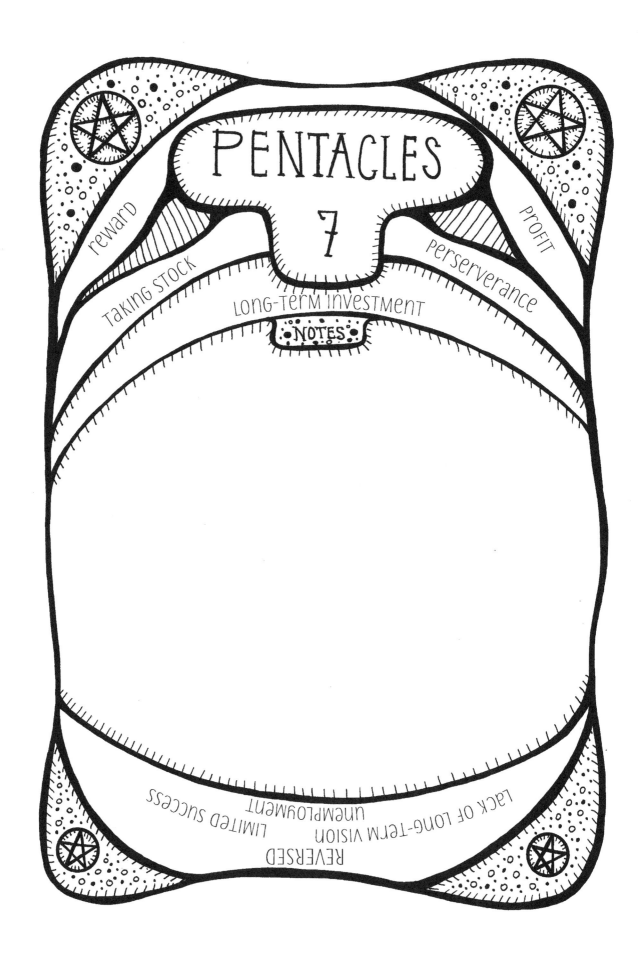

PENTACLES

7

reward

profit

TAKING STOCK

perserverance

LONG-TERM INVESTMENT

NOTES

REVERSED
LACK OF LONG-TERM VISION
LIMITED SUCCESS
UNEMPLOYMENT

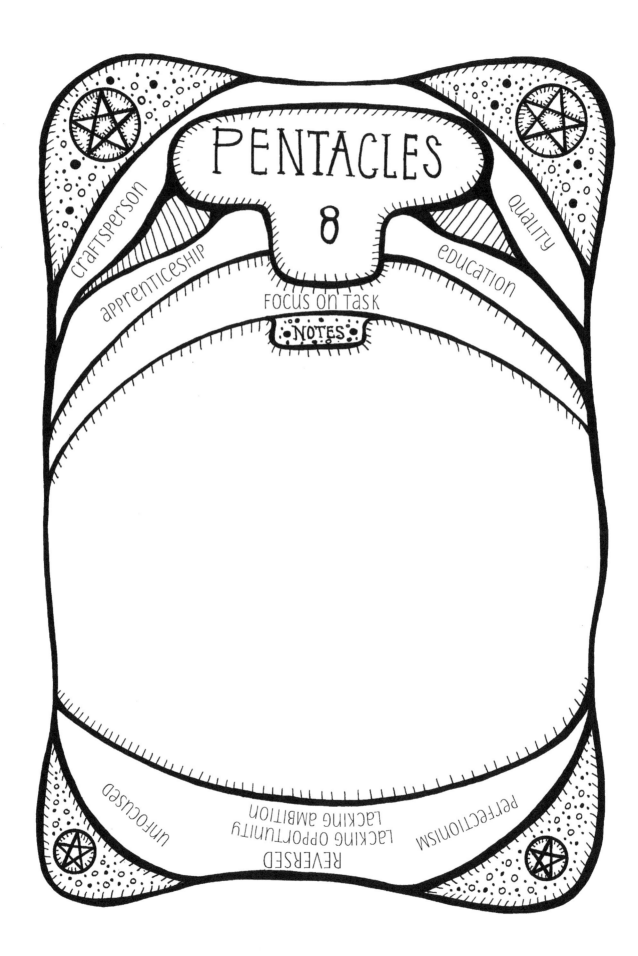

PENTACLES

8

CRAFTSPERSON
QUALITY
apprenticeship
education
FOCUS ON TASK
NOTES

REVERSED
UNFOCUSED
LACKING OPPORTUNITY
LACKING AMBITION
PERFECTIONISM

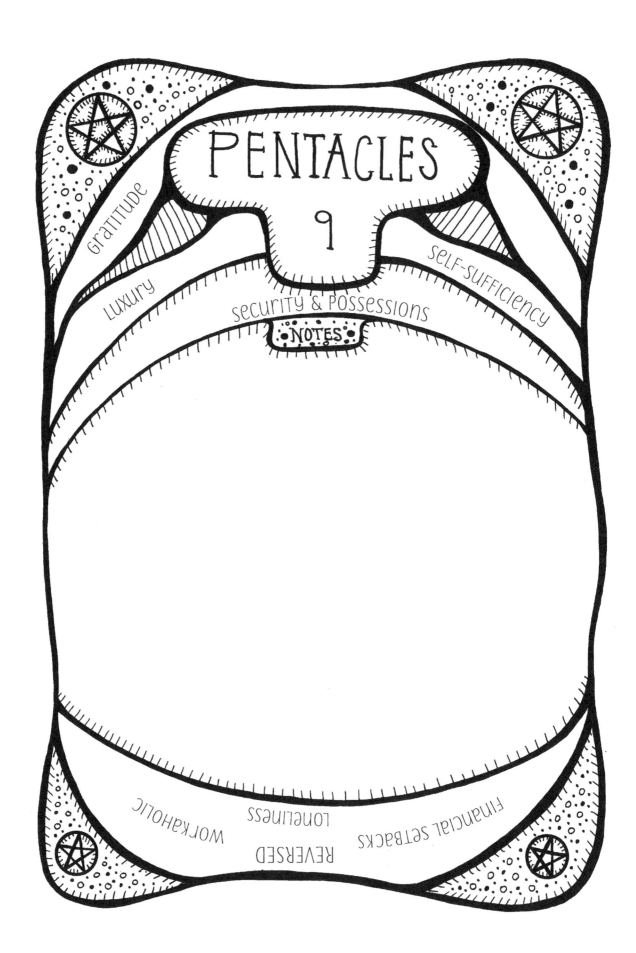

PENTACLES

9

Gratitude

Luxury

Security & Possessions

Self-sufficiency

NOTES

REVERSED

Workaholic

Loneliness

Financial setbacks

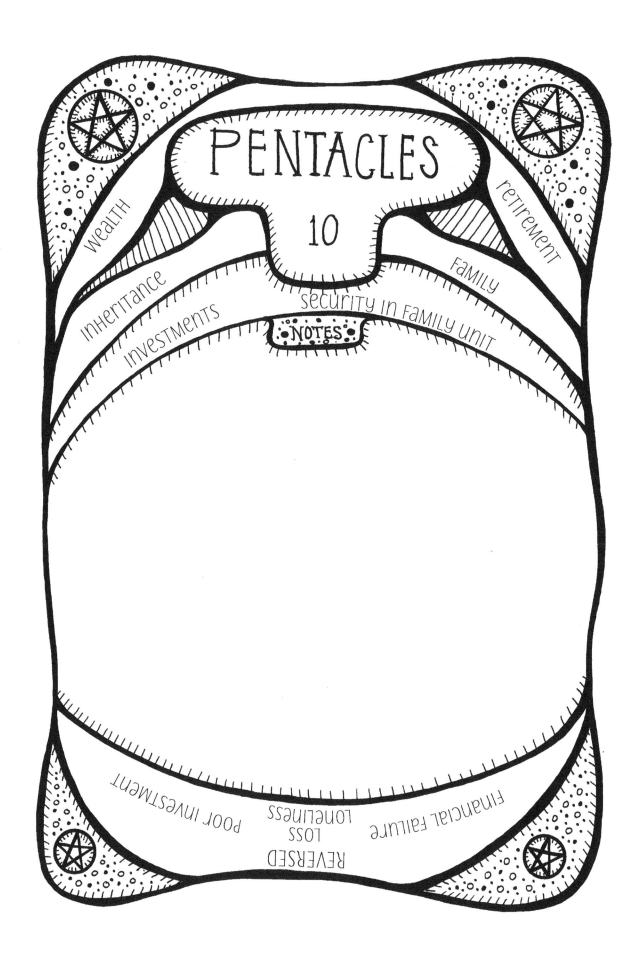

PENTACLES

10

WEALTH

retirement

INHERITANCE

FAMILY

INVESTMENTS

SECURITY IN FAMILY UNIT

NOTES

REVERSED

POOR INVESTMENT

LONELINESS
LOSS

financial failure

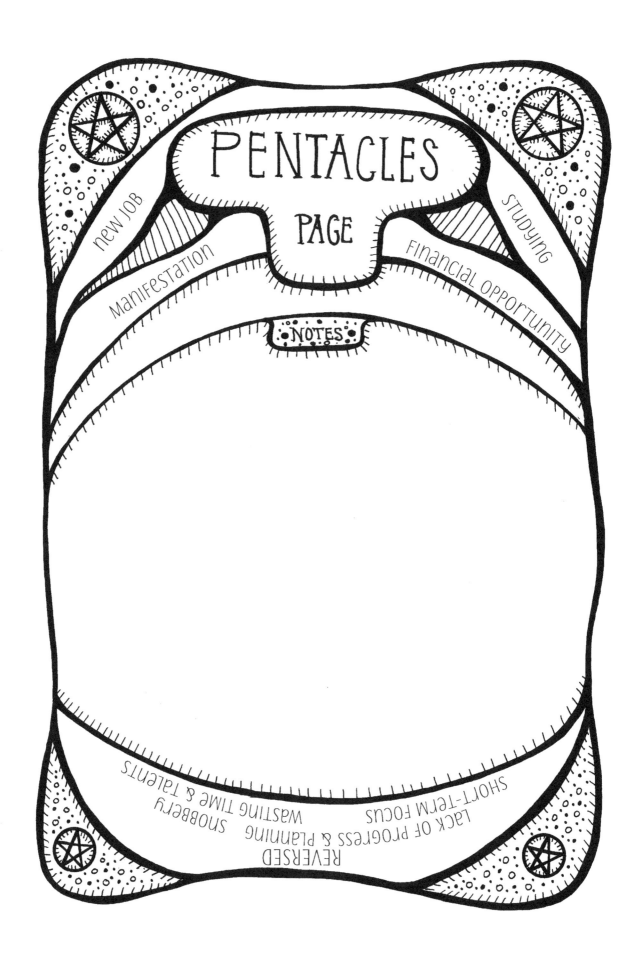

PENTACLES

PAGE

NEW JOB

STUDYING

MANIFESTATION

Financial opportunity

NOTES

REVERSED

Lack of progress & planning   snobbery   wasting time & talents   SHORT-TERM FOCUS

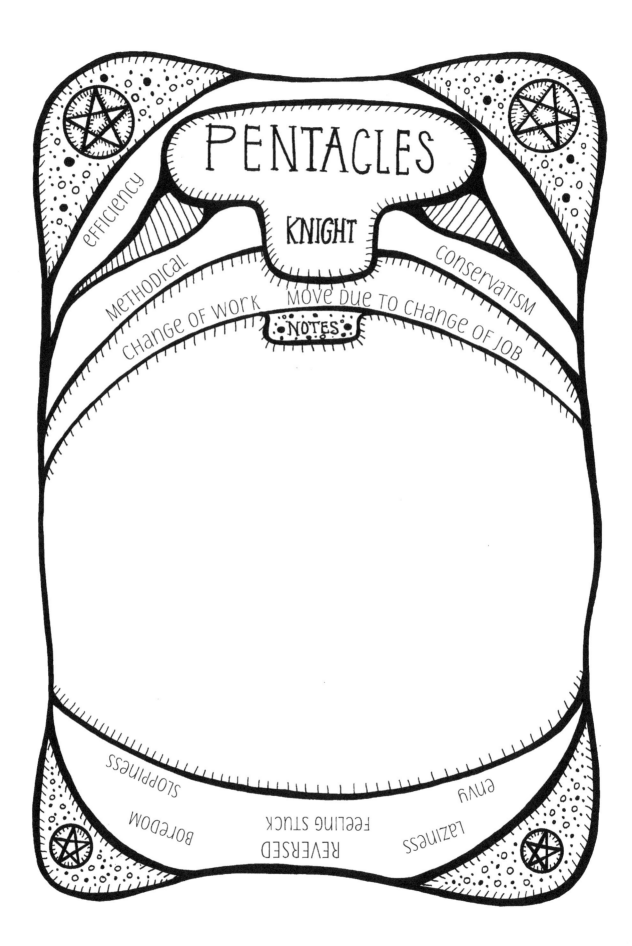

PENTACLES

KNIGHT

EFFICIENCY

METHODICAL

CHANGE OF WORK

MOVE DUE TO CHANGE OF JOB

CONSERVATISM

NOTES

REVERSED
FEELING STUCK

SLOPPINESS

BOREDOM

LAZINESS

ENVY

KNIGHT of PENTACLES

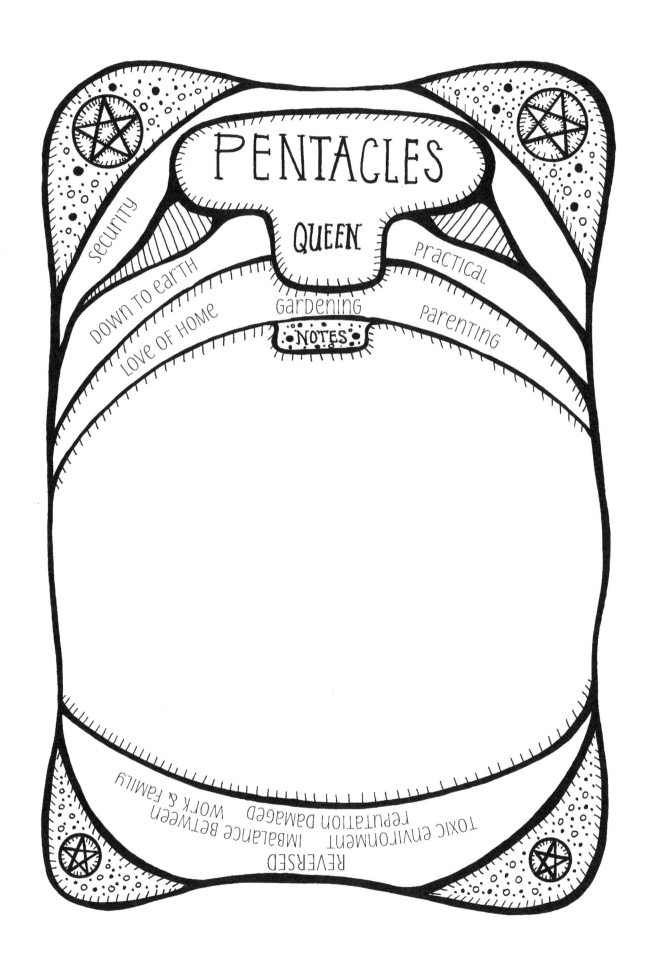

PENTACLES

QUEEN

SECURITY

DOWN TO EARTH

LOVE OF HOME

GARDENING

NOTES

PRACTICAL

PARENTING

REVERSED
TOXIC ENVIRONMENT   IMBALANCE BETWEEN   WORK & FAMILY
reputation damaged

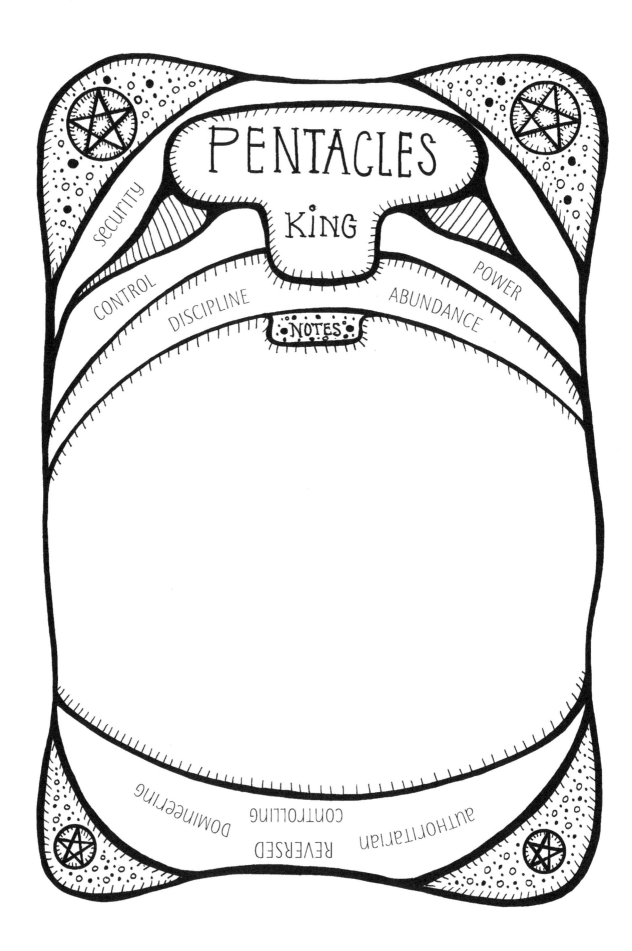

PENTACLES

KING

SECURITY

CONTROL

DISCIPLINE

POWER

ABUNDANCE

NOTES

REVERSED

DOMINEERING

CONTROLLING

AUTHORITARIAN

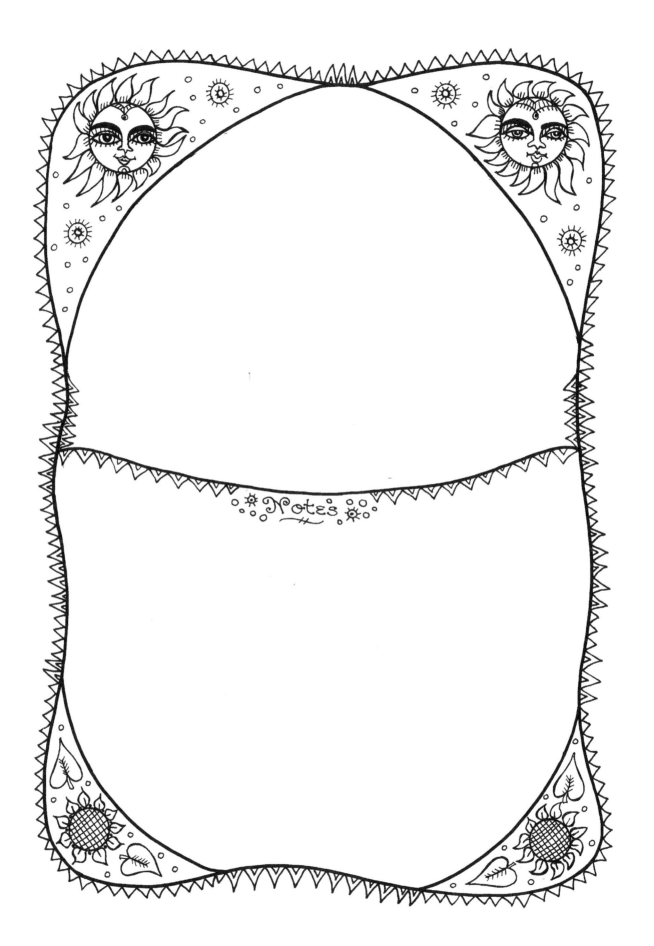

Notes

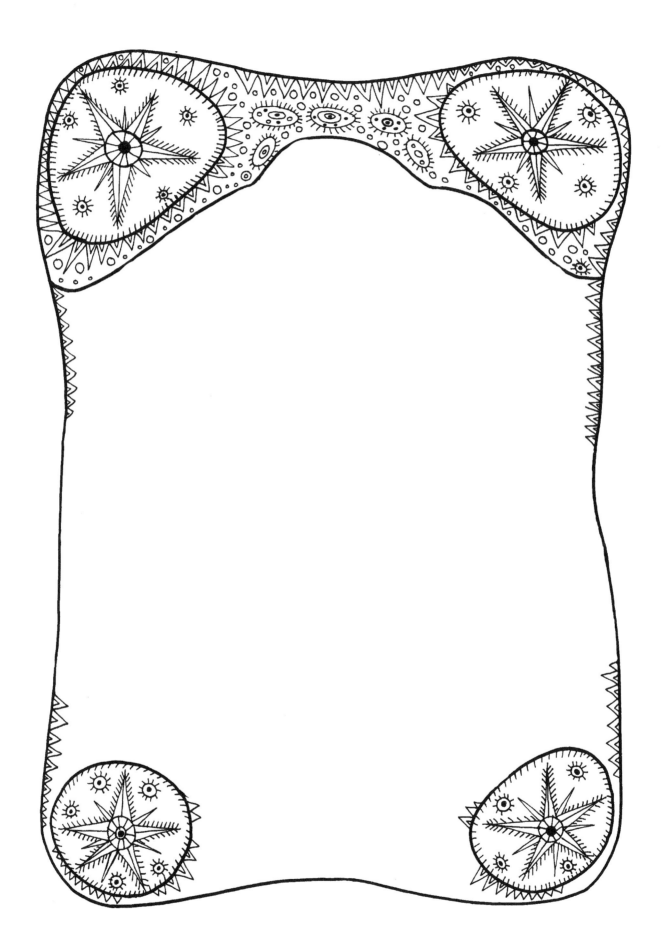

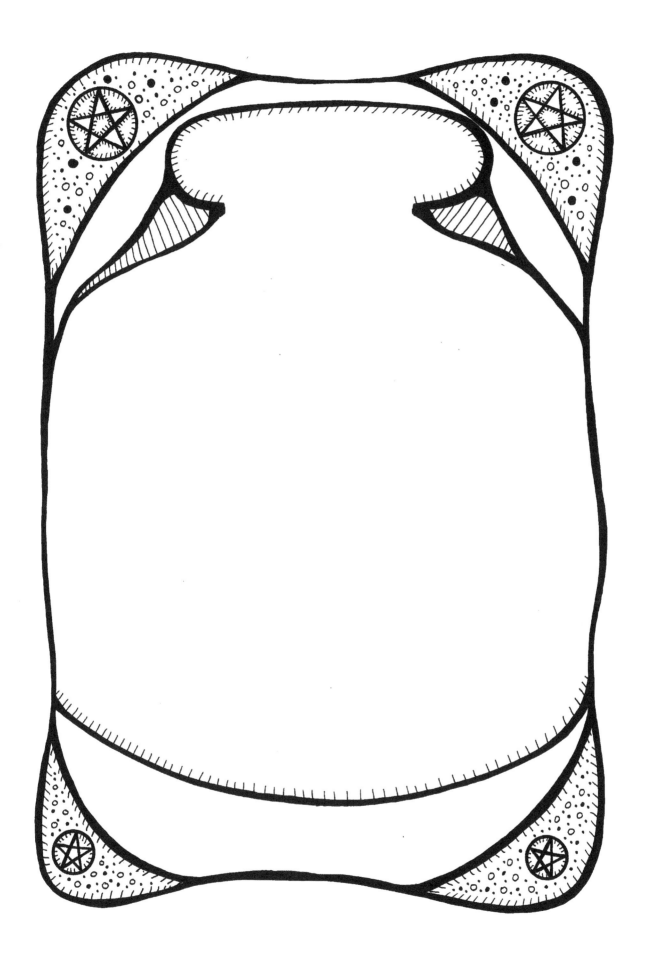

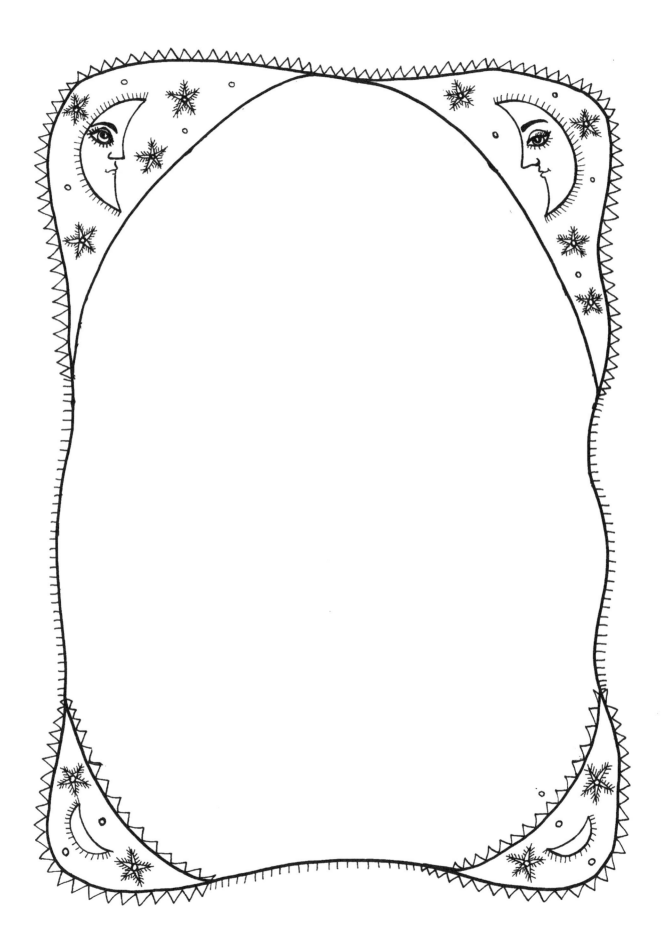

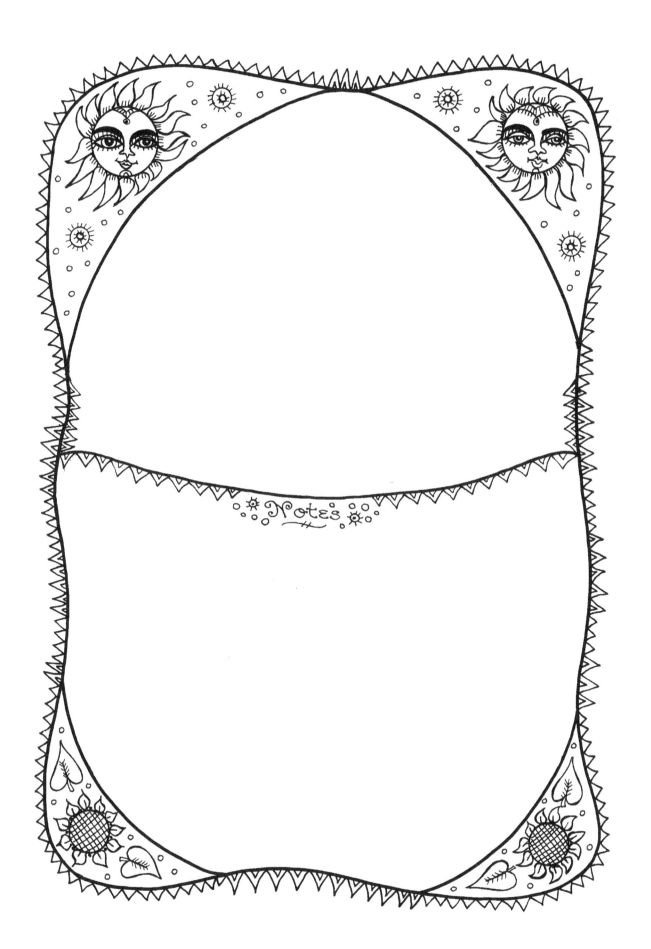

Notes

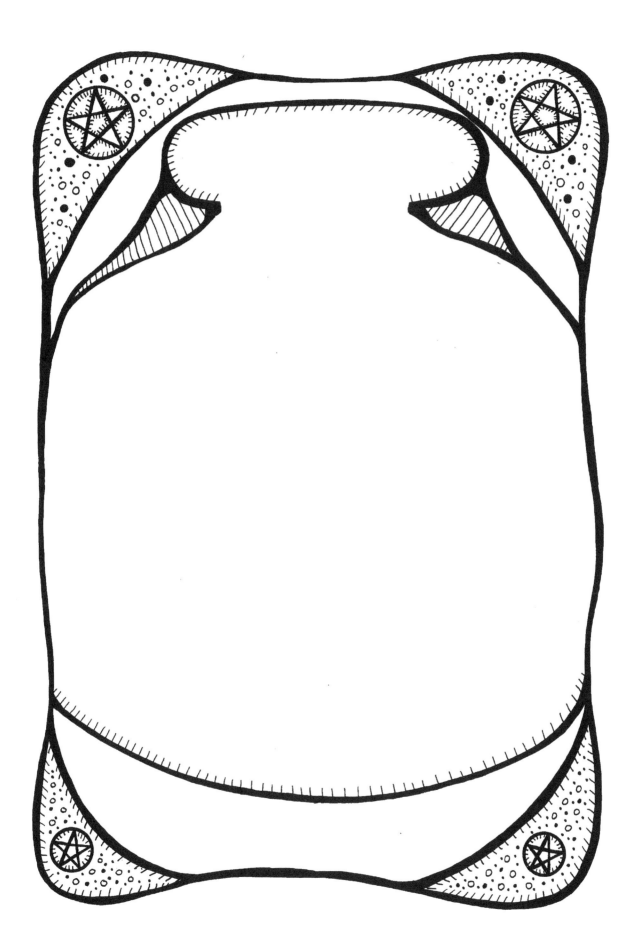

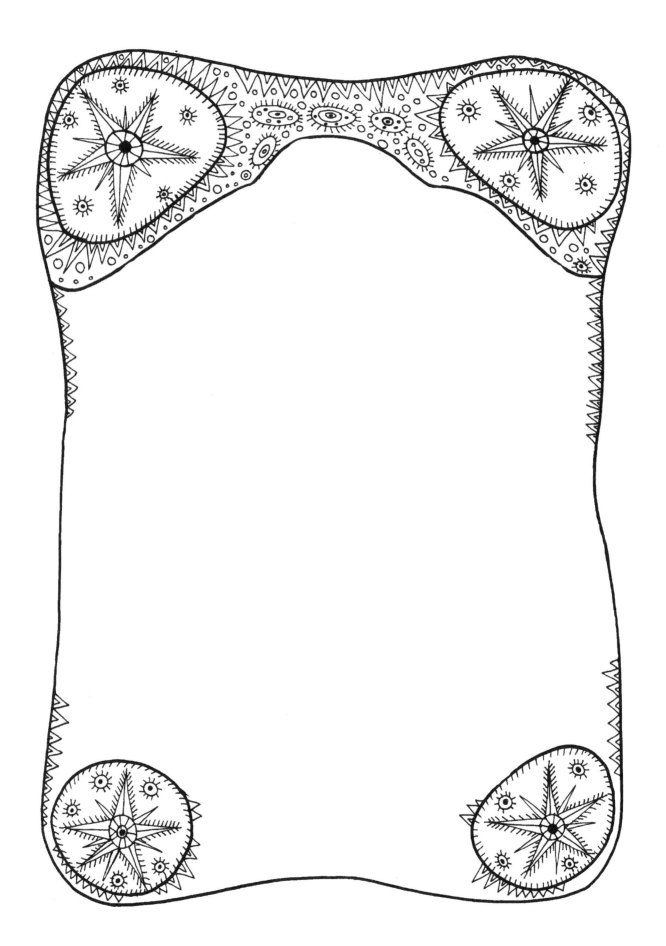

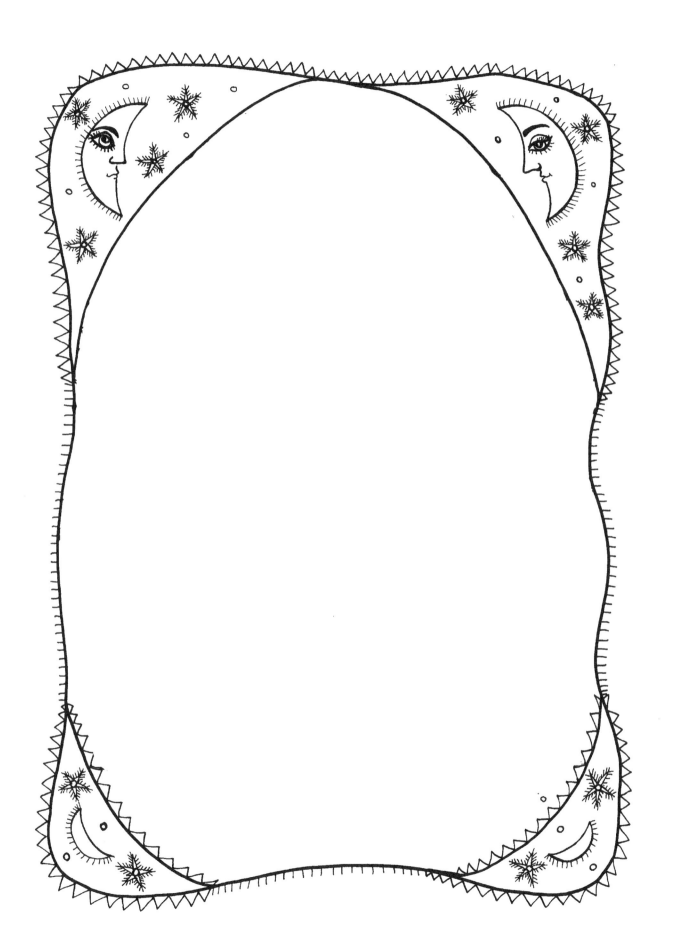

ABOUT THE AUTHOR

Diana Heyne is an American multidisciplinary artist, teacher, and writer currently living in France. Her family tree is rich in nature mystics, diviners, and creative folk who encouraged her in all these areas from an early age. Diana has had numerous exhibitions in the US and internationally, including miniature architecture in the New York Botanical Gardens popular annual holiday train show and a sculpted angel tree topper for the White House Christmas display. Her Etsy shop, Pandora Jane, is a widely recognized purveyor of natural materials, faery furniture, and houses.

TO OUR READERS

Weiser Books, an imprint of Red Wheel/Weiser, publishes books across the entire spectrum of occult, esoteric, speculative, and New Age subjects. Our mission is to publish quality books that will make a difference in people's lives without advocating any one particular path or field of study. We value the integrity, originality, and depth of knowledge of our authors.

Our readers are our most important resource, and we appreciate your input, suggestions, and ideas about what you would like to see published.

Visit our website at *www.redwheelweiser.com* to learn about our upcoming books and free downloads, and be sure to go to *www.redwheelweiser.com/newsletter* to sign up for newsletters and exclusive offers.

You can also contact us at *info@rwwbooks.com* or at

Red Wheel/Weiser, LLC
65 Parker Street, Suite 7
Newburyport, MA 01950